Finding Julia:

The Early Development of Southeast Missouri

Kaye Smith Hamblin

Southeast Missouri State University Press | 2014

Finding Julia: The Early Development of Southeast Missouri
By Kaye Smith Hamblin

Softcover: $15.00
ISBN: 978-0-9903530-3-4

First published in 2014 by
Southeast Missouri State University Press
One University Plaza, MS 2650
Cape Girardeau, MO 63701
www6.semo.edu/universitypress

Cover photo: Kaye Smith Hamblin
Cover design: Carrie M. Walker

Finding Julia:
The Early Development of Southeast Missouri

In memory of Julia Elizabeth Russell Harris and the Women of Bollinger: Pioneers of the Faith and Women's Rights

Table of Contents

Prologue:

The Historical Search For Julia

This book developed in a very roundabout way. In 2003, my husband Bob and I bought the century-year-old house at 313 Themis Street in Cape Girardeau. As we were moving in, our son Steve, a building contractor, remarked about the unusual room in the middle of the basement, but we were in the throes of moving and unpacking and quickly forgot about it. In the summer of 2009, I noticed that the lintels on the doorways leading in and out of the middle basement room have an arch made of two rows of brick, the type usually seen on outside doorways of old houses. The middle section, I observed, could easily have been divided into three small rooms. Could there have been a small brick house on the lot around which the present house was built?

For a possible answer to my question, I went to the Cape Girardeau County Archives in Jackson, Missouri. In the process of exploring tax books for the answer, the archivist told me about probate files. Once he placed in my hands the probate files for Joseph Russell and his daughter Julia E. Harris, the lady who with her husband built our house, I was hopelessly hooked on researching Julia.

In the probate folder I found Julia's will, which gave information about all the amazing real estate, bank shares, and other assets she had inherited from her parents; a record of her death in St. Louis, funeral arrangements, and her burial in Cape Girardeau; and also hints about her ancestors, the Bollingers and Russells, from whom she had inherited family heirlooms and property. I soon began delving into Missouri history books such as Louis Houck's *A History of Missouri*, Goodspeed's *History of Southeast Missouri*, Timothy Flint's *Recollections of the Last Ten Years in the Valley of the Mississippi*, Orenia Bollinger's *The Bollinger Connections*, Robert Douglass's *History of Southeast Missouri*, and Howard Conard's *Encyclopedia of the History of Missouri*. An archivist with the Episcopal Diocese of Missouri, Susan Rehkopf, recommended that I read *The Old Gravois Coal Diggings* by Mary Joan Boyer, which tells about the Russells of St. Louis.

Having grown up in Mississippi, I missed having a school course in Missouri history. As I began to find out about Julia's ancestors, I wanted to know the history of the time frame in which they lived, so

I investigated pertinent historical occurrences and anecdotes relating to the family and the Missouri history that they helped make.

The process of writing this book has been a delightful surprise to me, as it has taken me on many sidetracks. Each new book or place or person I explored opened up more places to seek information—many of which I had never known about. I have let the story of Julia take me wherever the next information leads, and it has been a wonderful trip.

~ 1 ~

Missouri: Territory to State

The Bollingers: Coming to Missouri

Bollinger

George Frederick Bollinger

married

Elizabeth Hunsucker

Born to George and Elizabeth

Sarah Bollinger

In 1799, a group of German settlers began the long trek from North Carolina to the Upper Louisiana Territory, thus establishing the historic family line of Bollinger in the land which would become Missouri. A century later, one descendant of that line would grow up to become Julia Elizabeth Russell Harris and would build a beautiful house on the property at 313 Themis in Cape Girardeau, Missouri.

Julia's maternal great-grandfather, who led the expedition, was George Frederick Bollinger, for whom Bollinger County, Missouri, as well as the nearby town of Fredericktown, is named. George's German ancestors first emigrated from Zurich, Switzerland, to Philadelphia, Pennsylvania, in 1738, then migrated down the Shenandoah Valley to Tryon County, later changed to Lincoln County, North Carolina. George was born there in 1770.

About 1796, George and a friend, John "Moose" Mussgenug, headed west, having decided to explore the land called Upper Louisiana. Upon arrival in Cape Girardeau they became acquainted with Don Louis Lorimier, the commandant of the post, who in 1795 had received a grant of 7,000 acres from the Spanish government. Lorimier persuaded Bollinger to return to North Carolina and recruit as many settlers as possible, promising as many as 640 arpens to each. The land was divided by a French format consisting of 1 arpen wide by 40 arpens long, an arpen being .85 of an acre. In order to settle in Upper Louisiana, Bollinger had to sign off that all settlers were Roman Catholic, since at that time the Spanish were still in control and allowed only Roman Catholics to live in the region. Those who came with Bollinger were members of the German Reformed Church; nevertheless, Lorimier allowed the settlers in because of his respect for Bollinger and because he wanted the population to grow.

When George returned to North Carolina, he met and became engaged to Elizabeth Hunsucker, marrying her in 1798, on her eighteenth birthday. George spent a year recruiting families to join him in the new land. On July 7, 1799, a baby daughter, Sarah, was born to the couple. In the fall of that year, George Bollinger, several of his brothers, and a large group of twenty families and friends, all of whose ancestors had also come to North Carolina from Germany and Switzerland, began their journey to Upper Louisiana. However, when the group was ready to travel to the new territory, Elizabeth became ill, and she and Sarah remained in North Carolina with her parents. Unfortunately, Elizabeth died without ever seeing the new land George was so excited about.

A family account of this journey in *The Bollinger Connections*, compiled by Orenia Bollinger, suggests that the group stocked their wagons and carts with an abundant fall harvest and headed west, with the goal to reach the Mississippi River in mid-winter when, hopefully, the river would be frozen for their crossing. The travelers were elated when they arrived at the river opposite the village of Ste. Genevieve in late December and found the river already covered in ice. The group set up a camp to wait until the ice was determined to be thick enough for the crossing. On December 31, 1799, the ice was measured at two feet thick. A few trial trips across the ice were made on foot and horseback, and finally with a wagon. Plans were made to cross the next day, January 1, 1800. The group of devout German Reformed Protestants gathered to pray for God's protection. The cracking of whips urged the oxen onto the ice. Everyone who was able walked, and the wagon drivers put a safe distance between each wagon. The crossing was made successfully, with a welcoming committee of Ste. Genevieve residents awaiting them on the other side. The band was happy to be able to replenish their supplies and share news from the East before continuing their trip on to the banks of the Big and Little Whitewater Rivers, where they found an abundance of trees and began building their log cabins. After the group settled in, Lorimier required them to form a militia, and they were organized under the leadership of Bollinger as major. In the War of 1812, Bollinger was made a full colonel.

Since George had learned the miller's trade by helping at his family's mill in North Carolina, he built a large mill on the Big Whitewater River, the streams of southern Missouri offering an almost inexhaustible supply of water power. The mill was a very important business. Customers came from as far as seventy-five to one hundred miles away, often bringing their entire families to camp out by the mill while waiting for their grain to be ground, which might be a few hours or even a day or so, depending on the line of customers. These trips provided an opportunity for the discussion of political, religious, or domestic issues. It was also a time to engage in recreational activities, horseshoe throwing being a popular one. Most customers who lived nearby brought their grain in a sack holding two bushels slung over their horse's back. Larger amounts would require an oxcart. There were rules governing the mills. Grain must be ground in the order received. The miller took from customers a prescribed toll: one-eighth of the grain for a water mill and one-sixth for a steam-powered mill. Water mills were required to grind at least four days a week.

The census taken on November 1, 1803, shows the Bollinger family with one white male, one white female, one Negro male slave, and one Negro female slave, as well as four hundred bushels of corn, seven hundred pounds of cotton, sixty pounds of maple sugar, seven horned cattle, and three horses.

Apparently from 1793, when Lorimier arrived in the territory, until 1806, his was the lone residence at what was known as "post Cape Girardeau," where he managed the civil and military affairs for the Spanish government. According to historian Louis Houck, when the U.S. purchased Louisiana in 1803, no villages in the Cape Girardeau district had been laid out. Territorial Governor William Henry Harrison proclaimed that since there was no site already established, he would order the court of Common Pleas and General Quarter Sessions to be held on the lands of Louis Lorimier at "Cape Girardo." Lorimier offered four acres of ground anywhere "between Thorn's creek and the Shawnee path (present location) plus two hundred dollars cash and thirty days' labor of a man to build the courthouse." In 1806, the town of Cape Girardeau was laid out and the seat of justice was located there.

However, a major problem soon developed. Not long after the land had become the property of the United States in the Louisiana Purchase, Lorimier's title to all of the land that had been given to him by the Spanish was disputed. In the days of the Spanish ownership, large grants of land had been given. Since the Spanish considered uncultivated wild land of no value, it was granted freely to all settlers and farmers. Only improved land was considered valuable. However, immediately after the Louisiana Territory purchase, even the uncultivated land increased in value by 200 percent. Just before the transfer took place in 1804, some French speculators and some Americans who had already settled in Upper Louisiana received large land grants from Spanish Lieutenant Governor Don Carlos DeHault DeLassus, who provided amply for his family and friends with concessions. Under the concession the grant was pre-dated to August 1799. But DeLassus had no power to grant these concessions. DeLassus was the last Spanish lieutenant governor of Upper Louisiana and oversaw the transfer of the Spanish territory to the French and to the Americans on March 9–10, 1804. The French flag flew only one day over St. Louis. These extensive land owners, including the Chouteaus of St. Louis and Lorimier of Cape Girardeau, became very important.

By the United States Act of 1805, possessors of grants must have been either the head of a family or twenty-one years of age, having inhabited the land grant prior to the first day of October 1800. Under the act, a board of three commissioners was appointed by President Jefferson to hear testimony and decide on the authenticity of the claims. George Frederick Bollinger appears in the Land Book of May 1, 1806, presenting his claim to the commissioners for two concessions from Charles D. Delassus. He made other claims as well on other dates. The greed for land led to violence in the courts on occasion, leading to the custom for judges to carry pistols into the court for their protection. Due to the high number of disputed claims, lawyers rushed into the new territory. Legitimate title to Lorimier's land would not be finally cleared until 1836.

Building the Settlements

In the first decade of the nineteenth century, the district was filling quickly, but the disputes over legal title to the land held by Lorimier had slowed growth in Cape Girardeau; thus the county seat

Bollinger Mill ca. 1871. *Photo courtesy of Jackson Heritage Association.*

was moved to Jackson where a new town was laid out. By 1818, Jackson had a total of three hundred residents. Rev. John Mason Peck, an itinerant minister and newspaper publisher, described Jackson during that time period as containing "sixty to seventy houses, five stores, two shoemakers, one tannery, two good schools, one for males and one for females." He also said that the residents of Jackson, predominately young men, were "more moral, intelligent, and truly religious than the people of any village or settlement in the territory." On the public square were built the first courthouse and jail, both of which were made of logs, along with the whipping post and pillory.

Rev. Timothy Flint, first a Congregational minister and later a Presbyterian minister, born in Massachusetts in 1780 and educated at Harvard, became an itinerant minister to the western territories of the Mississippi Valley. He had come to the area in the hope that the climate change would improve his fragile health. He wrote a series of letters to his cousin Rev. James Flint of Salem, Massachusetts, which were collated by the cousin into *Recollections of the Last Ten Years Passed in the Valley of the Mississippi*. The book, published in 1826, was very successful in the eastern United States due to the curiosity about life in the new territories. Flint described Jackson as "a considerable village on a hill, with the Kentucky outline of dead trees and dead logs lying on all sides in the fields." Flint had a different opinion of the local residents from that of Peck. He said that in the year that he spent there,

My time passed more devoid of interest, or of attachment, or comfort, or utility, than in any other part of the country. The people are extremely rough. Their country is a fine range for all species of sectarians, furnishing the sort of people in abundance, who are ignorant, bigoted, and think, by devotion to some favoured preacher or sect, to atone for the want of morals and decency, and everything that appertains to the spirit of Christianity.

Flint described in great detail the German settlement along the Whitewater. Upon attending a meeting in the woods, he found that there were about four hundred German people present, with not more than six people of English descent. The women were unable to speak English well, while the men, who could understand English, expressed themselves with a peculiar German accent. They had located their settlement "by the clear beautiful stream in the forest and, not having much contact with the outside world, were preserving their German peculiarities." He was impressed not only with their honesty, industriousness, and ability to establish an orderly farm, quickly becoming prosperous, but also that each farmer had his own distillery for making corn whiskey. Physically he described them as "large, stout, and ruddy-looking men and women."

An Earth-Shaking Experience
The years of 1811 and 1812 would have been unforgettable for the inhabitants of Cape Girardeau County. At 2:00 a.m. on December 16, 1811, the settlements were awakened by a violent earthquake later to be estimated of 7.7 magnitude, accompanied by a very loud noise, with lighter shocks continuing to occur until sunrise. Eliza Bryan, a resident of New Madrid District, gave an account in her letter to Rev. Lorenzo Dow. According to Eliza, the lighter shocks continued on a daily basis until January 23, 1812, when another quake (of 7.5) occurred which was as violent as preceding ones had been. The earth continued to be agitated, "visibly waving as a gentle sea," and on February 4, 1812, following another series of shocks, "a concussion took place so much more violent than those which had preceded it, that it was denominated the hard shock" (of magnitude 7.7). The atmosphere was dense with a black, sulphurous vapor. During these months of continuing shocks, the residents were fearful to stay in their houses and lived for twelve to eighteen months in light camps made of boards, only a few brave souls venturing back to their homes.

Because Eliza lived in the New Madrid District, she would have experienced even greater destruction than in the hill country to the north because of the sandy soil composition that amplified the shaking. She said the earth was horribly torn to pieces, with very deep fissures, some estimated to be eight to ten feet wide and twelve feet deep, some extending for miles, and spewing out sand, water, coal, and black vapors. The Mississippi River receded, forming a mountain of water which fell rapidly, breaking off groves of cottonwood trees with its force and sweeping boats inland. Many acres of land disappeared.

The Louisiana Gazette, reporting the news from Cape Girardeau on December 22, 1811, noted, "The concussions of the Earthquake which commenced at two o'clock on Monday morning still continue. We have experienced five severe shocks which split two brick houses, and damaged five brick chimneys in this place."

Later, on February 15, 1812, the newspaper reported again from Cape Girardeau that the concussions continued even more severely and lasting longer than preceding shocks. The article stated that "the ravages of this dreadful convulsion have nearly depopulated the district of New Madrid, but few remain to tell the sad tale, the inhabitants have fled in every direction. It has done considerable damage in this place by demolishing chimneys [*sic*], and cracking cellar walls. Some have been driven from their homes, and a number are yet in tents."

Another reference from the time is found in the church minutes of Old Bethel Baptist Church in Jackson, Missouri. It states: "On Monday at 3 o'clock in the morning a great and tremendous earthquake commenced which broke many places of the earth at New Madrid County. It continued shaking very hard all this winter."

The quakes were felt in almost the entire eastern part of the United States. Letters and newspaper accounts from the period describe effects of the quakes in the northeast, including New York, Massachusetts (where in Boston the quake rang the church bells), New Jersey, Washington City, D.C., on south to Georgia, Alabama, North Carolina, Tennessee, and down to New Orleans. *The Louisiana Gazette* reported in its March 14, 1812, issue that the December earthquake was felt in Charleston, New Hampshire.

Amazingly there were only two casualties in the area attributed to the earthquakes. But property damage was extensive. An act of Congress called the "New Madrid Claims" was passed in 1817, which allowed the victims who lost their land in the earthquakes to relocate to any unclaimed public lands in Missouri, not to exceed 640 acres.

The Territory of Missouri

George Bollinger arrived on the scene in a very historic time: the beginning of a new state. By the Act of 1812, the territory's name was changed to "Territory of Missouri," and a territorial government was established, which included a governor; a legislative council, whose members were chosen by the U. S. president; and a house of representatives, whose members served two-year elected terms.

Governor Benjamin Howard ordered an election for representatives for the first five Missouri counties: St. Charles, St. Louis, Ste. Genevieve, Cape Girardeau, and New Madrid. Chosen at this election as territorial representatives for Cape Girardeau County were Stephen Byrd and George Frederick Bollinger. The General Assembly met annually in private homes in St. Louis, the first one being held December 7, 1812, at the house of Joseph Robidoux.

The Johnson Collection in the Southeast Missouri State University Archives contains information about George's service to Missouri, as well as copies of correspondence between George and his contemporaries. Beginning with the year 1812, George contributed a large segment of his life to the new territory of Missouri as well as the state which followed. His positions included representing Cape Girardeau, New Madrid, and the Fourth District in various terms as territorial representative, a member of the Legislative Council, and a member of the senate, becoming the president pro tem in 1828. At the end of his terms he compiled a span of twenty-eight years serving his new state. George's grandson Samuel Daugherty would follow his grandfather's example as an elected state representative in 1860. However, as the Civil War began, the legislature was dissolved.

Louis Houck's book, *A History of Missouri*, gives a description of the process as Missouri developed to become a state. Some of the business done by the first territorial assembly involved making laws for weights and measures, establishing the office of sheriff, creating courts of common pleas, calling for a census of white males in order to establish representation, creating the Bank of Saint Louis, forming Washington County out of Ste. Genevieve County, and making provision for paying legislators. One of the issues of the second assembly, held in 1814, was making highways and roads, as it has been in every legislature since. The 1815 session set up two judicial circuits: Northern (St. Charles, Saint Louis, and Washington counties) and Southern (Ste. Genevieve, Cape Girardeau, and New Madrid counties). The Act of 1816 made the common law and statutes of England prior to James I the law of the land unless in conflict with laws and the constitution of the U.S. The fourth and final assembly created eight new counties and divided the courts into three circuits, along with adopting a memorial "praying for establishment of a state."

The memorial was first presented to the U.S. Congress on February 2, 1818, by the Honorable John Scott, one of the former owners of our property on Themis Street in 1811, who was the delegate sent to Washington from the territory. The memorial contained the reasons Missouri should become a state. First, the population had greatly increased to an estimated forty thousand citizens after the close of the War of 1812. Second, Missouri had passed eight years as a first-grade territorial government and five years as a second-grade territorial government. Third, the territory had supported the Union in the late war.

The memorial also listed four grievances:

The territory has no vote but is subject to taxation.

The veto of the territorial executive is absolute over the actions of the territorial legislature.

The Superior Court is the final authority on almost all controversies, without correction by any other entity.

The powers of the territorial legislature are limited to laws of a local nature since Congress has the ultimate authority.

The memorial was referred to a committee consisting of John Scott and one representative each from Kentucky, New Hampshire, Massachusetts, and Pennsylvania. As chairman of the group, Scott reported to the legislators a bill to "authorize the people in that territory to form a constitution and state government on equal footing with the other states." However, Nathaniel Tallmadge of New York presented an amendment which would put the condition in the bill that "further introduction of slavery or involuntary servitude shall be prohibited except for the punishment of crime, whereof the party shall have been fully convicted; and that all children born within the state after the admission thereof, shall be free at the age of twenty-five years." Missouri residents had an extreme objection to this condition, and it began a great debate which for the first time had the debaters divided by geographical lines. Threats of dissolution or civil war were issued. The debate continued through the winter. Finally, Tallmadge's amendment was passed 97–56 and then sent to the Senate. The Senate refused the amendment, the House would not compromise, and the session ended with the Union in a divided state and Missouri not being admitted.

The Sixteenth Congress met in second session in December 1819.

The subject of Missouri came up again, but this time Maine had also asked for admittance. The Senate suggested that the two admissions should be coupled. Otherwise, Maine would not be admitted. After more heated debate and a series of compromises, the "Missouri Compromise" was passed, and a bill was passed for the admission of Maine with an amendment allowing Missouri to organize the state by calling a constitutional convention. The bill also barred slavery in the territory north of parallel 36 degrees 30 minutes except in the boundaries of Missouri.

The intense debates had drawn such a deep line between those for slavery and the small number that wanted it abolished that no one who was not committed to continuing slavery could stand a chance of being elected to the state constitutional convention. Timothy Flint was in Missouri when the state passed from territory to state, and he recorded that the slave question was discussed with great vigor. Flint thought that the people from the western territory were more interested in being elected to office than in the East. In fact, he said that "electioneering is carried on with more unblushing effrontery." In this new government the people had a chance to gain a distinction for themselves. He went on to say,

> The campaign was hard fought. Much ink was shed. Many political essays came from the presses, which will never go down to posterity. But on the whole, that redeeming principle which seems to be mixed with the administration of government on American principles, brought about the issue with a quietness, which considering the bitterness of the competition, the nature of the case, and the elements of strife and discord which were so abundantly mixed in this chaotic political mass, was incredible.

Flint was present for the first two meetings of the convention and noted that a sign had been plastered around the speaker's chair saying: "Missouri, forgive them. They know not what they do."

Becoming a State

When the U.S. Congress met once again on November 13, 1820, Representative Scott submitted a manuscript copy of the new constitution to the committee, after which the committee reported that it "was republican and in conformity with the provisions of the Act of March, 1820." But the anti-slavery party seized upon the clause which required the Missouri legislature to enact a law "to prevent free Negroes and mulattoes from coming and settling in the state," and once again the whole country was in turmoil upon the question of admitting Missouri. On a motion by Henry Clay of Virginia, the question was referred to a committee of thirteen who were able to influence the legislators to pass the act of admission by adding the condition that the new state would not pass any laws to prevent any persons who now are and who may become citizens of the Union from settling in Missouri. On August 10, 1821, President James Monroe issued a proclamation declaring Missouri the twenty-fourth state of the Union. Thomas Jefferson, in a letter to John Holmes dated April 21, wrote,

> This momentous question, like a fire bell in the night, wakened and filled me with terror. I considered it at once as the knell of the Union. It is hushed indeed for the moment, but this is a reprieve only, not a final sentence. A geographical line, coinciding with a marked principle, moral and political, once conceived and held up to the angry passions of men, will never be obliterated; and every new irritation will mark it deeper and deeper.

His fears that the controversy over the compromise would eventually destroy the Union were indeed a forecast of things to come in the Civil War. At the time of the election, Missouri had 70,618 residents, of whom 11,234 were slaves. More than 1,000 of the slaves were in Cape Girardeau County.

Houck says that it seemed to him that if Congress had not tried to prohibit slavery in Missouri and the issue had been left to the people, that slavery would have been discontinued in the new state. However, Section 26 of the 1820 Missouri State Constitution stated:

> The General Assembly shall have no power to pass laws; first, for the emancipation of slaves without the consent of the owners, or without paying them, before such emancipation, a full equivalent for such slaves so emancipated; to prevent bona fide emigrants to this state, or actual settlers therein, from bringing from any of the United States, or from any of their territories, such persons as may there be deemed slaves.

Even so, the convention also added a clause that slaves should be treated with "humanity" by their owners, and owners should abstain from causing injuries to the slaves. Slaves were to have a right to trial by jury. Section 28 stated: "Any person who shall maliciously deprive of life or dismember a slave, shall suffer such punishment for the like offense as if it were committed on a free white person." Some historians seem to doubt that this part of the Constitution was honored in actual practice.

The Mormon War of 1838

From Jefferson City, the capital of Missouri, in December 1838, George Bollinger wrote to his friend Charles Welling back in Jackson. Charles was married to George's granddaughter, Elizabeth Frizel. In his letter, found in the State Historical Society of Missouri, George chides the family for not writing the news from home. He anticipates needing about two thousand pounds of pork, since he will have more workers the next season, and requests that Welling make the purchase for him.

George also comments on the Mormon War, saying: "We have had but little excitement, except when the Mormon War, as it has been called, has been up. This set all on fire. That is all from the seat of war in this neighborhood."

One of the major issues in Missouri at this time was the conflict between the Mormon and non-Mormon residents. According to documents in the Missouri State Archives, Joseph Smith, the founder of Mormonism, declared in July 1831 that the second coming of Christ was at hand and would take place at the town of Independence in Jackson County, Missouri. The announcement predictably caused a rush of Mormons to the location, the total number of those settling in Missouri during the next several years being over ten thousand. But the Mormons were found objectionable to other residents because of the large numbers moving in and because of their religious beliefs, particularly the idea that God had given them western Missouri for their Zion. The Mormons voted in blocs, to have political influence, and usually were abolitionists, moving to Missouri from the northeastern United States and Canada where that view was held in contrast to the slave-holding Missourians, who had mostly migrated from the South. The Missourians also feared that the large exclusive settlements planned by the Mormons would damage the economics of their towns.

Stephen C. LeSeuer has written a book about the conflict entitled *The 1838 Mormon War in Missouri*, which gives a very detailed look at the war, using original letters, journals, petitions, and official documents from the time. Most previous writings about the war have been written by and focus on the Mormons. By contrast, LeSeuer sought also to give attention to the Missourians, especially the non-Mormons who sought to stop the violence on both sides. LeSeuer states that "these new source materials offer interesting information and insights regarding the causes of conflict and the reasons why local authorities were unable to halt the violence."

By 1833, the first vigilantes had organized in Jackson County, where they attacked Mormon leaders, destroying their printing press and driving them next door to Clay County, where they were treated with kindness but nevertheless were expected by the Missourians to keep moving on. However, in 1836, the Mormons were still in Clay County and even more had arrived. LeSeuer quotes Missourian Joseph Thorp, a resident of Clay County, who said, "The Mormons told local settlers that this country was theirs [the Mormons'] by the gift of the Lord, and it was folly for them [the Missourians] to improve their lands, . . . that it would finally fall into the hands of the saints."

Clay County leaders David R. Atchison, Alexander W. Doniphan, and Judge Elisha Cameron sought to help the Mormons to find a new county of their own. Doniphan, who was a state representative, initiated the bill for the new Mormon county named Caldwell. The Missourians helped their new neighbors by allowing them to purchase on credit, lending them money to buy land, and even employing them. The Mormon journal, *The Elders' Journal*, reported that "the Saints here are at perfect peace with all the surrounding inhabitants, and persecution is not so much as once named among them."

In 1838, however, the "perfect peace" began to erode. The Missourians believed that the Mormons had agreed to settle only in Caldwell County, but as over five thousand new Mormon settlers arrived, they began to create large settlements outside their county of Caldwell, moving into Daviess County and laying out a new town to be called Adam-ondi-Ahman, meaning, according to Joseph Smith, "the place where Adam dwelt." They also began to plan for even more new towns in other counties. Some of the strict members of the Mormons created a secret society called the Danites to insure conformity to church rules, using force when necessary to drive dissenters from the Mormon land. The Mormons also became aggressive and belligerent against Missourians, all of which led to an atmosphere of fear and distrust.

After a tentative peace broken here and there, a skirmish broke out on August 6, 1838, at the Gallatin Election Day. It was the first-ever election to be held in Daviess County, and the older settlers realized that the Mormons, because of their superior numbers, could determine the outcome. When non-Mormons attempted to prevent Mormons from voting, a fight broke out and escalated, ending with many wounded but no fatalities. After this incident, both factions began to organize militia troops, and greatly exaggerated stories and rumors abounded.

The book *Mormon War Letters Written in 1838 by Missouri Militia Officers and Citizens* contains many of the letters posted to Govenor Lilburn Boggs, as well as communiqués to and from military officers. On October 13, Captain Samuel Bogart of the volunteers pleaded with Boggs, "I hope you will take steps to make a final settlement of this matter. If it is not done soon, our country is ruind [*sic*]." On October 9, Major General Atchison urged Boggs to come to Carroll County to restore peace. William P. Penniston, Company G, wrote to Boggs on October 21: "They [the Mormons] have robbed and burned every house in Gallatin, our county seat, among the rest our Post Office . . . [and] have driven almost every individual from the county flying with their families through snow without necessary clothing . . . They have burned for me two houses." H.G. Parks, 2nd Brigade, 3rd Division, wrote to Major General Atchison, "The excitement in this county is more deep and full of vengeance than I have yet seen it, and I would not be surprised if some signal act of vengeance would not be taken on these fanatics." In a sworn report, Jonathan J. Dryden told about being taken prisoner by the Mormons, but being released due to illness. His captors stated they had asked Govenor Boggs for protection, to which he gave no response. Therefore, they were taking the law into their own hands, plundering and burning homes in the countryside of Daviess, and driving non-Mormons from their homes to recover their losses in Jackson County. The non-Mormon citizens of Daviess and Livingston Counties also called on the governor for protection. Their letter states that the Mormons were preparing for a "war of extinction."

The Battle of Crooked River

The Battle of Crooked River on October 25, 1838, grew out of an attempt by the Mormons to rescue three of their company who had been taken prisoners by the Missourians. The Mormon leaders quickly gathered a troop of fifty and left during the cover of night to free the prisoners. About 3:00 a.m. they dismounted and marched to the camp where they encountered a sentry who fired into the soldiers, hitting one of them. The Missourians were alerted by the shot and scrambled from their tents to take up places behind the river bank. The Mormons charged the Missourians, who panicked and ran for the river. The news from the Battle of Crooked River gave out many different reports. One Mormon estimated twenty to thirty Missourians killed, while another soldier thought the total was forty to fifty. They believed the company was nearly destroyed, but the actual total was one killed and six wounded. The Mormons' casualties were three killed and seven wounded.

Lilburn Boggs, governor of Missouri during the Mormon War. *Public domain photo.*

First reports by the Missouri Militia said that almost all had been killed, others reported ten dead and the rest taken prisoner; however, the soldiers had fled the scene so fast they had no idea what had happened. A letter from Sachel Woods and Joseph Dickson to the governor stated: "We were informed last night by an express . . . that Captain Bogard and his company of between fifty and sixty were massacred by the Mormons . . . (except three) . . . Our county is ruined, for God sake give us assistance as quick as possible." The barrage of letters after the battle caused Governor Boggs to muster 2,500 state militia to end "the Mormon insurrection." The order relieved Major General Atchison of his command and placed General John G. Clark in charge. In a letter to General Clark, Boggs said he had just received from his aides

> information of the most appalling character which entirely changes the face of things and places the Mormons in the attitude of an open and avowed defiance of the laws and of having made war upon the people of this state. Your orders are therefore to hasten your operations with all possible speed. The Mormons must be viewed as enemies and must be exterminated or driven from the state if necessary for the public peace.

This became *Missouri Executive Order 44*, subsequently known as the "Extermination Order." In the next session of the legislature, Atchison condemned the order, saying the governor had no authority to make such a proclamation. Nevertheless, this extermination order remained on the books until Governor Christopher Bond rescinded it on June 25, 1976.

The Mormons gathered their troops as well as their families in the two strongholds of Far West and Diahman, while the troops assembled by Govenor Boggs's order moved toward the town of Richmond for the final showdown with the Mormons at their town of Far West. On the morning of October 31, Major General Lucas received a message from Colonel Hinkle, who commanded the Mormon troops, requesting a meeting to find a way to avoid using arms. While awaiting word from Lucas, Joseph Smith received news of the massacre of the Mormon families by militias at Haun's Mill, and he realized that the Mormons must obtain a treaty to protect his people against annihilation.

The Mormons Surrender

When Hinkle and Lucas met, Lucas read the governor's order, shocking the Mormons with its severity. LeSeur quoted John Corrill, one of the Mormon leaders, who said, "I expected we should be exterminated without fail. There lay three thousand men, highly excited and full of vengeance . . . and now they had authority from the executive to exterminate." Lucas promised no more bloodshed if the Mormons agreed to the terms laid out. He required that the Mormon leaders surrender to be tried and punished, that all the Mormons give up their property to pay for the damage done by them, that the Mormons should leave the state with the state militia providing protection, and that they should give up their arms. On November 1, the 2,500 troops paraded to an area south of Far West under a show of force and formed a hollow square. Then the 600 Mormons formed another hollow square inside the larger square where they surrendered their arms. The leaders, including Joseph Smith, were arrested and taken to Richmond for trial.

On the night of the surrender, a court martial, which was illegal since the Mormons were civilians, was called by General Lucas to try the seven leaders of the group. Joseph Smith and the other leaders were sentenced to be shot, but General Doniphan, the officer in charge, refused to carry out the sentence, saying, "It is cold-blooded murder. I will not obey your order." The leaders were not executed.

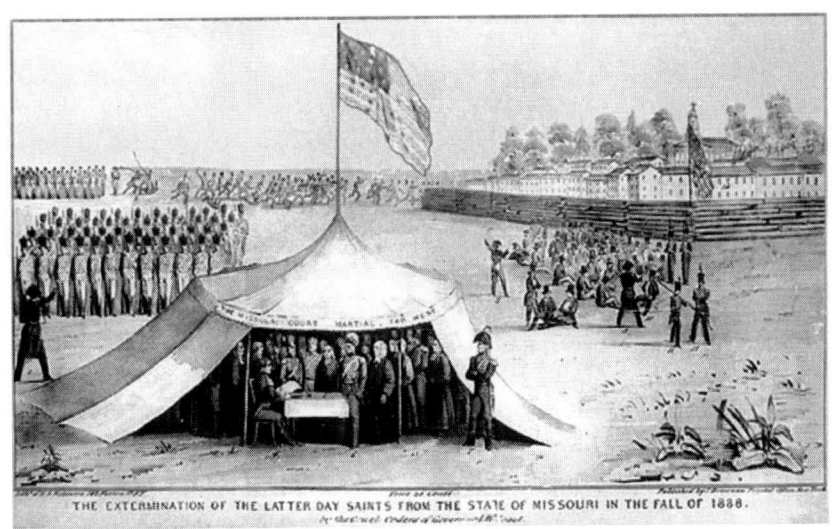

THE EXTERMINATION OF THE LATTER DAY SAINTS FROM THE STATE OF MISSOURI IN THE FALL OF 1838.

Conclusion of Missouri Mormon War, 1838. *Photo courtesy the* Daily Missouri Republic, *November 9, 1838.*

The next day, five hundred Mormons were required to sign over their property.

The Richmond Court of Inquiry began November 12, lasting until November 29, trying sixty-four Mormon defendants. Their trial included three areas: the raids in Daviess County, which included plundering and burning; the battle at Crooked River; and an accusation of treason. There were forty-one witnesses, twenty for the Missourians and twenty-one for the Mormons. Judge King held twenty-four defendants to stand trial on suspicion of arson, burglary, robbery, and larceny; five others who were charged with murder; and Joseph Smith plus five others who were charged with treason. Surprisingly, he released the other twenty-nine with no charges. It was a one-sided trial with no investigation of the Missouri vigilantes who drove the Mormons from their homes, plundering and burning, or the Missouri militia who committed the massacre at Haun's Mill.

The *Southern Advocate* newspaper located in Jackson, Missouri, ran a series of articles dealing with the crisis in the northern part of the state. The September 1, 1838, issue describes efforts of the citizens of Carroll County to remove "Mormons, abolitionists, and other disorderly people" from Carroll County. The writer goes on to say that they are citizens of Missouri and entitled to the rights of the state. And that the best remedy is to let the law take care of the problem. However, by November 10, 1838, opinions had changed. The writer then described the Mormons as the "band of infuriated fanatics" who defied laws, plundering and burning, and published a letter from Judge Austin A. King, the judge of the circuit where the Mormons lived, who gave a detailed description of the situation. The November 17, 1838, issue tells the readers about the capture of "Joe Smith" and four hundred other Mormons. The article ends with this statement: "It is said that they are fast leaving the State: and this in our opinion is their best policy."

Since there was obvious wrong done on both sides of the issue, the state legislature called for an impartial investigation into the matter. The Senate members voted to appoint a committee to investigate, while the House opposed it. George Bollinger was appointed to the investigative committee, which consisted of six members from the Senate and six from the House. The bill was postponed until the next session beginning in July. By that time most of the Mormons had left the state, and no investigation by the state legislature ever took place. George concluded in his letter to Charles Welling, "My own opinion is that there has been some of the very worst kind of conduct on both sides, and more than likely when investigated will not add much to the credit of our State." Doubting that any good would come from an investigation by the legislature, he went on to say that thirty to forty of the "poor deluded Mormons" had been arrested for treason, arson, murder, and larceny. In December the legislature passed a bill setting aside two thousand dollars for relief of Mormons and anti-Mormons who lost their homes in the conflict.

The Mormons Leave Missouri

The final issue, which was debated in the newspapers, as well as in the state legislature, was whether or not the state had a legal right to expel a group of its citizens. The question was settled by popular opinion as the majority was in favor of expulsion.

With the disarming of the Mormon soldiers came a surge of plundering and violence by the Missourians. The soldiers killed the farm animals of the Mormons for food as well as sport, ransacked the homes taking anything they wanted, and inflicted beatings on the men. There were some unverified reports of rape of the women. The last requirement of the Mormons to remove themselves from Missouri was still to be met. General Clark told the Mormons they could wait and leave in the spring; however, they were so unbearably mistreated that those who could left, even though winter was coming, forcing them to travel through snow and ice. They crossed the Mississippi River into Quincy, Illinois, arriving in abject poverty, but citizens there took them in and provided for their needs.

Meanwhile, Joseph Smith and the others held for treason were imprisoned in the Liberty Jail, and during their trial were indicted for the crimes charged against them. Interestingly, serving on the jury was Robert Penniston, whose home was burned by the Mormons, and Jacob Rogers, who killed a Mormon at the Haun's Mill massacre. Because the new judge had been the prosecuting attorney at Richmond, the prisoners were granted a change of venue to Boone County. When they stopped for the night, the prisoners were allowed to escape, eventually reaching Quincy. By May 1839, nearly all the Mormons had left Missouri. No Mormons were convicted of crimes committed during the war. At the end of the war, Mormons had twenty killed and twenty wounded, while the Missourians had one killed and twelve wounded.

LeSeuer feels that "most people in both groups tried to follow a peaceful and moderate course, but rumors, prejudice, fear, and misconceived devotion to God carried the conflict beyond the control of its participants, leading normally law-abiding citizens to commit numerous crimes." Research brought LeSeuer to several conclusions about the Mormon War. First, the majority of the Missourians were not as prejudiced against the Mormons as history has indicated. Second, Joseph Smith was responsible for encouraging the militant and lawless activities of the Saints, including the plundering and burning of non-Mormon homes. Third, the cause of the Mormon dissenters' disagreement with the church was their opposition to the militant and criminal actions of the Mormons. Fourth, the Richmond Court of Inquiry was a preliminary hearing to gather evidence as to whether the defendants should be held over for trial, and was not a "mock trial."

LeSeuer points out that although Mormons who committed crimes were punished, the non-Mormons remained free. The Mormons were denied their right to live where they wished, similar to other groups who conflict with community norms and have been denied their rights. In the state of that time, the law was in the hands of the local people, with an unreliable peace-keeping force, and the acceptance of vigilantes. The state upheld the notion of majority will by giving in to the vigilantes' demand for expulsion of the Saints from their counties. LeSeuer feels that when the state gave in to the vigilantes' demand, the "outcome of the Mormon War was shaped by a powerful American tradition of adherence to the principles of democracy and majority rule, which often superseded principles of fairness and the rule of law."

Suits filed against the federal government for compensation for losses due to the war, the cost of which was about one million dollars, were denied because of a strong states' rights policy in the United States.

Correspondences of George Frederick Bollinger

The correspondences of George Frederick Bollinger found in the Johnson Collection give an indication of some of the other issues that the legislature addressed. From that collection comes a letter written on December 20, 1840, from Thomas B. English in Jefferson City to Major Bollinger, giving an account of transactions in the legislature. Reading the goings-on in the capital is like reading the headlines of current newspapers as English describes the problems facing the government. The new officers of the bank have been elected with most of the old directors voted out since they "seemed to have dipped rather deep in the funds of the institution." The debt for the Mormon War has not been paid off; the Osage and Iowa troops are wanting their pay; the State Capitol, under construction, will require fifty or sixty thousand dollars to be finished; and the Bank is in a "strait," having put up collateral for the state bonds at 50 percent discount to meet liabilities. English adds, "In short we are heels over heads in debt and in trouble."

A letter dated November 20, 1832, informs George that he had been chosen an elector for the fourth district of the state, which meant that he would be voting in the presidential election to determine whether Andrew Jackson would have a second term as president with Martin Van Buren on the ticket for vice president. Missouri's four electoral votes went to Jackson. This was the first election in which the political parties selected their nominees in a convention.

From Washington City, D.C., in a letter to George Bollinger, U.S. Senator L.F. Linn on May 6, 1842, speaks to a claim from Bollinger for "labours [sic] and expenses in defence [sic] of his neighborhood," which was presented to the proper committee and refused on several occasions because the defenses were made by a private citizen without the approval of the public officer authorized to make such contracts. The issue of the claim was first mentioned in a letter to Bollinger, addressing him as "Respected Friend," written on October 19, 1834. Salutations in other letters include "My Dear Friend," and "My Dear Major."

Linn also reported:

> in the apportionment bill the house have deemed it proper to assume a power which if not questionable, has been dormant for fifty years—they have provided that every state in the Union *shall* adopt the district system in electing their representatives to Congress. This I think will give rise to much discussion in the Senate. The quarrels between the two divisions of the Whig party continue and the breach seems to increase with the lapse of time—this, at least you can rely on as a fact.

Three letters, dated March 19, 1836, January 8, 1838, and January 8, 1839, address the establishment of "Post Routes" and the suggestion of Bollinger for the mail routes. Linn is preparing a general plan for the whole state. The 1839 letter promised that a check for Bollinger's pay as a mail contractor would soon be in the mail. He also referred to the news from Bollinger about the prospects of a stage coach route running from Fredericktown to Farmington to St. Louis. Linn closed with the words, "Send my kindest regards to your excellent daughter [Sarah Bollinger Daugherty] and for your self assurances of high regard and Friendship."

Senator Lewis F. Linn, a U.S. senator from Missouri for ten years, was also called the "Iowa Senator" because of his concern with the Iowa Territory. Linn County, Iowa, as

U.S. Senator L.F. Linn from Missouri and friend of George F. Bollinger. *Photo courtesy of NYPL Digital Gallery.*

well as Linn County, Missouri, is named for him. *The Iowa Historical Record* credits Linn as being the most influential man of his day in encouraging the immigration of Americans to Oregon. Beginning in 1841, he annually introduced a bill in Congress to establish American jurisdiction over Oregon, offering the enticement of 320 free acres of prime Willamette Valley land to white male settlers and American Indian half-breeds, age eighteen or older. His bill, the Donation Land Claim Act, was finally passed on September 27, 1850, which began the "Great Oregon Migration." Once the bill was passed, settlers were required to arrive before December 1, 1850, in order to receive the land. If they were married before that date, their wife could also claim 320 free acres *in her own name*, which was most unusual at that time. Linn City in Oregon is named for the senator.

The Johnson Collection also contains letters to Bollinger from William McDaniel and Dr. I. Curl, dated September 1838, regarding the three men's having been appointed by Governor Boggs to serve on a committee to "examine into the general state and condition" of the Bank of the State of Missouri at St. Louis and Fayette. The committeemen sought to arrange dates for the bank examinations in order to travel to St. Louis and Fayette to complete their reports by the time the legislature met again on November 17. A later letter dated February 8, 1841, from James Russell, a Missouri state legislator, was written to Bollinger to give him the news that legislative approval had been given for the location of a third branch of the state bank in Jackson, something for which Bollinger had lobbied for a long time. Russell reported the difficulty presented by the members from the "Mineral Region" as well as the "northwestern boys" who were trying to locate the new bank in Lexington.

As these summaries indicate, the Bollinger letters in the Johnson Collection provide a revealing index into significant political, economic, and social developments of that period.

~2~

Slavery in the Territory:

The Beginning of Slavery in Cape Girardeau County

In his book *The Slaves and Slave Owners of Cape Girardeau County*, Edison Shrum compiled extensive information and statistics on the topic. He states that an old map of the Spanish land grants that were granted prior to 1803 shows that the largest group of claims belonged to the families who came to the area with George Frederick Bollinger. In the 1830 census, eight of the settlers owned fifty-five slaves among them. George Bollinger's property list upon his death in 1842 included thirty-four slaves at a value of $12,725.

The slaves were important for clearing the land, farming and growing the food crops, and building and operating the mills, as well as building the homes of the settlers: log cabins at first and later much more substantial houses. There were also roads and bridges to be built in the new land. Male slaves were given training in such skills as carpentry, blacksmithing, millwrighting (dealing with the construction and maintenance of machinery), and stonemasonry. The women slaves were usually domestic workers such as cooks, spinners, seamstresses, weavers, and caregivers for the children. Timothy Flint described the abundance of dresses hanging in the room in which he slept when visiting with one of the Bollinger families: "I counted forty-five female dresses hung round my sleeping room, all of cotton, raised, and manufactured, and coloured in the family."

Most families in Southeast Missouri who owned slaves had only one family of slaves, and the greatest majority of owners in Cape Girardeau County seldom had more than seven slaves. The Cape Girardeau County tax records for 1856 show that the largest slaveholder had forty slaves. The master of the farm and his sons usually worked alongside the slaves doing general farm work, as did the mistress in doing the housework, in contrast to the system used on the large plantations in the South, with an overseer driving hundreds of slaves in huge fields.

Strangely enough, before the Revolutionary War, England was

sending such a large number of slaves to the colony of Virginia that the planters requested that the slave trade be discontinued, but the king refused because of the wealth the trade brought to the crown. After the war, about 1794, the United States began to make laws to stop the importing of slaves. By 1820, most imports had ceased, the need for new slaves being met by the children being born into slavery. As the slave-holding settlers from the East began migrating to the Missouri Territory, they brought their slaves with them. There was acceptance of slavery from the beginning of settlements in the Louisiana Territory and in the Missouri Territory, as well as when Missouri became a state. In fact, most of the early lawmakers had come from slave states in the southeast and owned slaves themselves. Shrum points out that perhaps due to the legal right to own slaves, people like the Byrds, Ramseys, Bollingers, and Buckners came to Cape Girardeau County, and by being able to bring their slaves with them, were able to clear land, build houses, barns, mills, roads, bridges, etc., much more rapidly than would have been the case had they not had slaves to assist in this work.

Shrum also suggests that Bollinger's slave workforce made it possible for him to devote his energies and time to developing the territory and state as he served in the territorial assembly as well as the state legislature and state senate.

The holding of slaves became a very prevalent practice in Cape Girardeau County, including a complete cross section of the population who were slave owners. Every mayor of Cape Girardeau from the first mayor until the Civil War, when the city was occupied by the Union Army, had slaves. Slaves were owned by medical doctors, teachers at the Cape Girardeau Academy, and merchants, as well as by the owners of flour mills, sawmills, woodyards, tanyards, flour and grist mills, a furniture manufactory, and a wagon-making shop. Ministers were a surprising addition to the list. John H. Clark, a prominent Cape Girardeau County Baptist minister, owned sixteen slaves, and Thomas Parrish Green, a pastor at Old Bethel Church as well as the founder of the Cape First Baptist Church, owned one slave in 1828 and three in 1830. Also owning slaves was Father John M. Odin, a Catholic priest and later bishop at Saint Mary's Seminary in Perryville, who owned twenty-seven slaves (1830). D.E.Y. Rice, a Presbyterian minister, owned two slaves, and Benjamin Benefield, a Methodist minister in 1860, had sixteen slaves. St. Vincent's College in Cape Girardeau and Saint Mary's Seminary in Perryville were owners of slaves.

An exception to those in favor of slavery was William Daugherty, a staunch abolitionist. William was married to Elizabeth Ramsey, the daughter of Andrew Ramsey, the first settler in the Cape Girardeau district just outside Lorimier's grant. Ramsey left his daughter an inheritance that included seven slaves, thereby creating a problem for William. He would not own slaves but allowed those inherited by his wife to stay as servants rather than send them out on their own.

One of the most interesting stories found in the abstract of our lot at 313 Themis is that of Alfred P. Ellis, who bought the lot on February 3, 1835. He owned twenty-seven slaves in 1828 and twenty-nine in 1830. His will, which was probated on June 12, 1841, directed that his wife, Fannie Ellis, and son-in-law, Ignatius Wathen, be appointed the executors of the estate. The request was made by the executors that such real estate as was necessary should be sold to pay outstanding debts but that the slaves should not be sold, with the exception of Sam and Ann, who were ordered by the sheriff to be sold "in the town of Cape Girardeau at public sale on the 25th day of December next." Other owners of the lot who were slave owners were Jeremiah Abel (one slave in 1828); James Fulkerson (five slaves in 1830, two in 1840); Charles G. Ellis (seventeen slaves in 1828); and Joseph Russell, the father of Julia Russell Harris, who owned seventeen slaves in 1850.

The founders of Jackson, Ezekiel Able and his son-in-law William Ashley, who owned the land, as well as the first commissioners, John Sheppard, Samuel G. Dunn, Abraham Boyd, and Benjamin Shell, were all included in the list of slave owners. The first courthouse at Jackson, destroyed by fire in 1819, was replaced by a brick structure in 1837. The builders of the successive courthouses were all slave owners and would undoubtedly have used their slaves in the construction of the buildings. Slave owners also included the members of the board of trustees of Jackson, the town constable, the operator of a saddlery shop, blacksmiths, a hatter, carpenters, merchants, court judges and lawyers, and bankers. Virtually all of the newspaper owners, teachers, and educational facilities in Cape Girardeau County owned slaves.

In addition to slave auctions to settle estates being held at the courthouse, on the courthouse grounds also stood a whipping post. One whipping took place at twelve noon on November 28, 1845. Four slaves had pled guilty to breaking and entering the home of Johnson Ranney, a Jackson attorney. Their penalty upon conviction was thirty-nine stripes on their bare backs. Interestingly, the penalty for a white man for breaking and entering in the first degree would have been not less than ten years in prison, and for second degree not less than three years. However, to enforce that severe a penalty on slaves would have been a penalty against the owner as well.

Slavery and Old Bethel Church

Apparently there was no stigma or guilt involved in being a church member or even a church officer and owning slaves. Records show that the following officers of Old Bethel Church owned slaves in 1830: Isaac and John Sheppard, deacons; Wilson Thompson, pastor from 1812–1814; James and William Wilkerson, deacons; William Mathews, singing clerk; Robert English, clerk; and Thomas Parrish Green, pastor, 1818–1826. William Hill, clerk, was the only church officer not holding slaves.

The Bethel Church Book, Minutes of Proceedings 1806–1867 indicates that slaves were welcomed into the membership of the Old Bethel Baptist Church. Various entries show the professions of faith as well as church discipline of their Negro members along with the white members. Some examples from the minutes of the proceedings are shown below:

> October 11, 1806 : The Church met in conference. Agreed to build a meeting house on Thomas Bull's land. Received by Baptism Mr. Byrd's Negro woman Vicey.
>
> March 12, 1808: Received by experience a negro woman named Hannah, belonging to Mr. Russell.
>
> October 10, 1813: Mr. Byrd's Negro Vicey excluded for telling a falsity and for refusing to hear the church.
>
> June 13, 1818: The committee agree that the black members have the seat behind the white male members at all times, to which the church agreed.
>
> August 7, 1819: Vicey, Mr. Byrd's Negro woman, excluded from the church, came forward to be restored, laid over to next meeting.
>
> September 11, 1819: Vicey's trial voted out.
>
> July 8, 1820: Application made by Vicey for her restoration. Agreed to reconsider her case next meeting.
>
> August 12, 1820: Vicey's case taken up, and she left to write to Sister White and Hannah if they can fellowship her, and the church to wait their answer.
>
> September 8, 1824: Sister Violet, a black member, died September 8. She belonged at her death to Mr. Moses Byrd.

September, 1824: Dismissed by letter, Sister Terry, a black sister belonging to Sister Rebecca Randol. (Note: The letter would be presented to another church where it would serve as proof of the former church membership and profession of faith.)

August, 1834: Brother Dick Green, a black man age 103, departed this life in 1834.

Laws Governing Slavery

A document from the Missouri State Archives describes the "Laws Concerning Slavery in Missouri: Territorial to 1850s." The attempt to maintain control of the slave population in the area that became Missouri began as early as 1682 during the French and Spanish colonial period and lasted until the Civil War. Before the black slaves were brought to the territory, Indian slavery was common in the territory. Indians who were captured during tribal wars were sold to the white traders. The first black slaves were brought by the French to the lead mining area of the territory in 1720. The French developed the "Code Noir" (Black Code), which covered punishment for a slave "striking a master or other free persons, leaving their master's property without permission, or carrying guns or owning property." Owners also had guidelines. They were instructed not to torture, mutilate, or kill their slaves, but were seldom punished for doing so. When selling slaves, owners were prohibited from breaking up a slave family with children under age fourteen. Many, however, ignored this law by not recognizing slave marriages as legal. Miscegenation was also forbidden; however, this law was obviously ignored as the number of mulattos increased.

In October 1804, as Missouri became a territory, the legislature added a section on slaves in the laws of the district. The laws of the Code Noir were kept, with new regulations being added. Slaves were forbidden to participate in riots or unlawful assemblies or to make seditious speeches. Punishment was public whipping. Slaves could not engage in commercial business without permission of their owner. More laws came with Missouri's being granted statehood. In 1825, the assembly defined a black person as one with one-fourth part Negro blood, which made the person subject to all the laws that applied to slaves. Also, slave patrols were formed to monitor the movements of the slaves. The patrols had authority to administer up to ten lashes to a slave away from his plantation without a pass from his master or mistress. In the 1830s, fines were added for the owners who allowed their slaves too much freedom. Basically, the patrols were used to control the slave population by fear. When abolitionists became more prominent, an act was passed to prohibit the dissemination of abolition doctrines. Because an uneducated slave population made white citizens feel less threatened, the teaching of Negroes or mulattos to read or write was banned in the state.

The article closes with this statement:

> What began with the Code Noir of the French and Spanish colonial period continued over a half-century after the United States purchased the Louisiana Territory and eventually carved out Missouri. The black code measures promulgated and retained by these various governments constrained the slave and free black population and theoretically created a near-total system of control. In a slave society, slaveholders considered it necessary to monitor the daily lives of their slaves, thereby subjugating an involuntary labor force, and limiting the freedom of free blacks, who might otherwise agitate, and create unrest and rebellion among the slaves.

Another law governed the emancipation of slaves. First, an owner could emancipate his slaves by his last will and testament or in writing with two witnesses and registration in the circuit court. Second, this emancipation would make the slave perfectly free as if born free. Third, an emancipated slave could be taken by a person who was owed a debt by the former owner and required to work until the debt was cleared. This law was enacted in order to keep slave owners from trying to avoid a debt by freeing the slave. Fourth, the emancipator was responsible for the continued care of the emancipated slave if the slave was not of sound mind and body, if the slave was older than age forty-five, or if the slave was a male under age twenty-one or a female under age eighteen. Finally, the slave must receive a certified copy of the document granting his freedom.

Shrum gives some examples of slave emancipations in Cape Girardeau County. On March 21, 1805, Edward F. Bond manumitted his slave Mathew and gave him "full permission and liberty to go where he pleases and to do and to act in all cases as a free man." On February 5, 1858, Thomas Johnson emancipated Charlotte, age forty-eight, and her child, Susan, age two-and-a-half, with the added provision, "that said Thomas Johnson be held liable for the support and maintenance of said Charlotte and Susan so set free."

In 1850, the census showed that Frank J. Allen was a wealthy landowner in the Jackson area, owning a thousand acres of land, sixteen slaves, and several houses, including one in Iowa and a brick house in Jackson, five hundred dollars worth of farm machinery, and many horses, mules, oxen, cattle, and hogs, as well as an abundant harvest stored away. On March 4, 1846, Allen emancipated Mary, age twenty, and her children Elizabeth, age three, and Albert, fifteen months. Then on November 5, 1852, Allen manumitted his slave Sam, who was found to be "between ages 21 and 45, able bodied and sound of mind." After Allen freed his slave Jefferson on June 2, 1855, nine days later, Jefferson, now a free man of color, manumitted his slave Ellen, who was found to be "young, able bodied and sound of mind." There is no verification of the "rest of the story," but perhaps the romantic version is that Jefferson earned the money to purchase Ellen so that he might free her and they could be a family. Another similar case was that of Nicolas Dorsey, a colored man, who emancipated a Negro woman named Polly, who had been a slave of Robert Smith and had been purchased by Dorsey.

Allen's will stated that his slaves, Bob and John, who were in California, should be emancipated, along with Maria and her children (Sarah, Emily, Juliann, Elizabeth, Henry and Louis) and Sylvia and her children (Jefferson and Frank Allen). In a codicil dated April 10, 1857 (Allen died less than a month later), he left his slave, Lewis, age about eighteen; Rebecca, twenty-four; John, infant of Winney; and Toby, about twelve, to his wife Eliza with instructions that Toby should be freed at age twenty-one and Emily at age twenty. If Toby and Emily died before reaching the specified age, Eliza should take two of Maria's female children, with the exception of Sarah.

These slave owners were freeing the slaves that might have brought up to a thousand dollars each if they had been sold. In most cases they were found to be young, able-bodied, and sound of mind as the law required and would still have been productive workers. In the case of Thomas Johnson, he was still liable for the support of Charlotte and Susan even though they were no longer his slaves.

Another law forbade slaves to be forced to work on Sunday, except for regular housework or for charity. A master was fined one dollar for every so-employed slave. On February 28, 1853, R.R. Rollins of Boone County was fined five dollars for working slaves on Sunday.

Hiring Out of Slaves

Many slave owners had more slaves than they could use for their available labor.

Often widows, orphans, or other family members became slave

owners through inheriting slaves and chose to keep them as an indication of family prestige or as an investment, hiring them out to others requiring extra workers. In many wills, estate settlements, and contracts, arrangements were made by which the owner's slaves could be hired out to support underage heirs or widows, or sometimes simply to provide cash income for the owner himself. Rates for an adult slave ranged from $75 to $100 a year, with the employer responsible for food, clothing, medicine, and the fee paid to the owner. The hiring out of slaves owned by an estate which was still in probate was required to be overseen by the court, with the hiring being done once a year at the courthouse door and going to the highest bidder. The owner was responsible for paying taxes on the slave, as well as caring for the slave in old age. Of course, when hiring out his slave, there was the risk of injury to the slave or the chance to escape.

In 1914, Harrison Anthony Trexler published *Slavery in Missouri, 1804–1865*. At that point in time, he was still able to interview firsthand many people, including former slaves, who experienced the period of slavery. Trexler tells of one older slave from Liberty who recalled being hired out. The usual clothing allowance was "two pairs of trousers, two shirts, and a hat the first summer, a coat and a pair of trousers in the winter, and two pairs of trousers the second summer. The slave was clever enough to go to his new employer in his worst rags in order to get the full quota of clothing." A female slave told about her conditions as a hired-out slave. "I was hired out by my mistress, a widow woman, for one dollar a week and had to keep house for a family of seven. I was fed very badly." The rate paid for hire of men was about one-eighth of the valuation of the slave, while the rate for women was about one-sixteenth. The average price for house servants was $150 for males and $75 for females for a year. Slaves who were working on the river boats, as hemp hands on the farms, in livery stables, as mechanics, and as carpenters brought a higher rate for hire. They might bring $200-$250 for a year's hire. The Code of 1804 forbade an owner from allowing his slave to go about as a free man and hire himself out. The owner could be fined and the sheriff could hold the slave in jail until the next court term, when the slave could be sold after twenty days of advertising. Often the hired-out slave would be given a horse and allowed to return to the owner's plantation to visit his family at night if distance were not too great. Otherwise, he could return only on Sunday.

According to Shrum, in 1846, Thomas H. Walker was declared incompetent to manage his property, including forty-five slaves, which he had inherited from his parents, Andrew and Lucy Walker. Andrew's will of 1843 states his wish that "my negroes be made as to let them be amongst their children and connections." Charles Welling was appointed the guardian of Walker and his slaves and managed the rental agreements. In the 1850 census, the slaves seem to have been rented out to families in the area. The 1863 Cape Girardeau County Tax Book shows that Charles Welling was managing the slaves of six estates in addition to the Walker estate. In 1870, after the war had ended, several former Walker slaves were living with white families in Jackson, including two with Mattie and Linus Sanford, one with the Wellings, and one with the Sheppards. The Johnson-Ranney family had Nancy Jr. and her five children, while Nancy Sr. resided with the McFadden family.

The year 1863 was the last year that the Cape Girardeau County tax books listed slaves as taxable personal property. No longer were slaves sold for $800 to $1,000 each as at the highest point in 1859, but were $100 or less. Sarah Daugherty was listed with four slaves valued at $400 total. John Cross's slaves went from forty-seven slaves valued at $18,800 in 1859 to thirty-seven slaves valued at $7,400 in 1861 to fifteen slaves valued at $1,500 in 1863.

When the state convention met in St. Louis in July 1863, the members passed a resolution to gradually free the slaves by July 4, 1870. (On January 11, 1865, the delegates to another state convention led by Charles Drake passed the resolution for the immediate emancipation of all slaves in Missouri.) The end of slavery was approaching.

~3~

The Family of Bollinger

Sarah and Joseph Frizel

Frizel

Joseph Frizel

married

Sarah Bollinger

Born to Joseph and Sarah

Elizabeth Bollinger Frizel   Mary Langdon Frizel

Sarah Josephine Frizel

George Bollinger's daughter Sarah was an interesting person. Her father has been described as "generous, large, and powerful, a man of great energy and enterprise," and it is evident that Sarah inherited some of her father's traits. The 1803 census shows that Sarah, age four, had joined her father in Upper Louisiana. When Sarah was a young girl, she spent time with the Lorimier family when her father was away. Years later she described Lorimier's house, located in Cape Girardeau down by the Mississippi River, for Major James F. Brooks, who made a drawing of the house according to Sarah's remembrance. Major Brooks was an engineer who laid out railroad routes in Southeast Missouri. (*The Southeast Missourian*, November 8, 2010, mentions his completion of the route for the Charleston and Hickman Railroad, which would connect Cape Girardeau with Hickman, Kentucky, via Charleston, Missouri.) Sarah recalled the dormer window and the railing around it on the front of the "Red House," the Lorimiers' home, where she and Mr. Lorimier sat, and he held her in his arms to watch for a flat boat he was expecting on the river. She recalled that the front rooms were not built in the American style, but

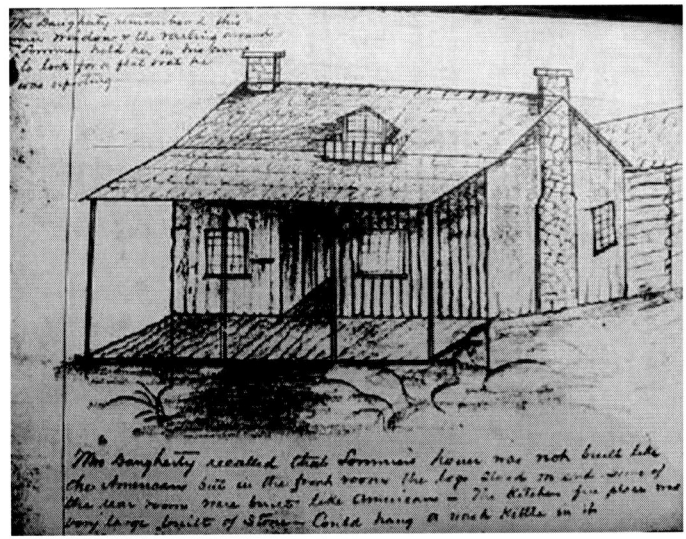

Sketch of Lorimier's "Red House," drawn by Major Brooks. *Photo courtesy of Cape River Heritage Museum.*

had logs standing on end. The rear rooms, which were added on, were designed with the more common horizontal logs. The huge kitchen fireplace, made of stone, could contain a wash kettle.

As a young lady, Sarah returned to Salem, North Carolina, making the trip on horseback, with her clothing in saddlebags, to attend a Moravian Seminary boarding school for girls. The curriculum consisted of the usual academic subjects, but also included such skills as needlework, housekeeping, spinning, weaving, ribbon work, sewing, tambour work, and knitting.

In 1816, the first pianoforte was brought across the river to the new settlement for Sarah, who apparently became an accomplished pianist. Sarah's pianoforte, a smaller version of the modern piano with only five octaves, is on display at the historic Oliver House Museum in Jackson, Missouri. According to Kyle Mabuce, member of the Jackson Heritage Association and a docent at the museum, Sarah's father paid $1,000 for the pianoforte, which was made by the Astor and Norwood Company of 79 Cornhill, London, England. Translated into today's economy, $1,000 would be about $11,000. The instrument was shipped from England to New York. From there it traveled to Philadelphia, where it was hauled by oxen to the Ohio River and put on a keel boat for its trip on the Ohio and Mississippi Rivers to Cape Girardeau, where once again it was hauled by oxen to its final destination in Whitewater. When the settlers and their families came to the mill on weekends to have their grain ground, on Saturday nights Sarah would play the pianoforte and provide the music for dancing and socializing in the mill. The instrument was donated to the Jackson Heritage Association in 1970 with only one leg attached, but it has been restored with the other three legs being made to match. Apparently the instrument also survived a house fire.

On January 25, 1819, Sarah was married to Joseph Frizel, who was from Wincasset, Maine. About 1805, Frizel had opened a mercantile store in St. Louis, later moving his business to Jackson, Missouri, where he was one of the original merchants, continuing in the business until his death. Joseph built a house for his new bride Sarah at what is now 209 West Main Street in Jackson. The house was built in a local version of a Cape Cod with kitchen in the rear, probably quite a contrast to the other log cabin style homes in the village.

Upon his arrival, Joseph had sought to have an Episcopalian minister come to the new territory. By the next year Reverend Thomas Horrell arrived in Jackson, having migrated from Maryland. However, since his wife was not very fond of frontier life, they soon moved to St. Louis. Frizel did not live to see another minister in the area. In 1821, due to a serious illness, Joseph was forced to sell the house, and the family moved to the Bollinger home on the Whitewater in hopes that would improve his health. His mother, Mary Langdon Frizel, who had come to Missouri from back East, was his nurse. However, he died in September 1823, leaving Sarah a widow with three young children under the age of three. Sarah and Joseph were the parents of Elizabeth Bollinger Frizel, Mary Langdon Frizel, and Sarah Josephine Frizel.

The old family Bible belonging to Mrs. Mary Langdon Frizel, Joseph Frizel's mother, contained detailed information about the children's births. The information was copied by her great-granddaughter, Mrs. Annie Guild W. Medley, into the record book at the Cape Girardeau Christ Episcopal Church.

Births

Elizabeth B. Frizel born January 31-1820 Monday 9 oclock in morning Jackson Missouri Territory.

Mary Langdon Frizel born July 28-1821 a little before 12 oclock Friday evening

Sarah Frizel born Feb 23-1823. After the death of her father, Josephine was added to her name.

Jan 23-1825 the children were baptized by the Rev. Wm Horrell

Elizabeth Bollinger Frizel
     Mary Langdon Frizel
     Sarah Josephine Frizel
     Joseph Daugherty born May 3-1832

Note by granddaughter: "M.L. Frizel came here from Boston and located in Jackson and is buried in family burial ground Burford-ville."

Joseph Daugherty was the son of Sarah Bollinger Frizel and Ralph Daugherty, whom she married after Joseph Frizel's death.

Joseph Frizel's funeral was conducted by the Rev. Dr. Thomas Horrell from Christ Episcopal Church in St. Louis, who stated in his diary that he "rode a horse from St. Louis to Jackson September 4, 1823. Baptized Mary Frizel and sister after reading funeral service at the grave of their father." Horrell returned to Jackson in 1825 with his wife, four children, and six slaves. The Bollinger and Frizel families supported his ministry in the county, where he held services at his home and also in Cape Girardeau.

Sarah Bollinger's piano. *Photo courtesy of Jackson Heritage Association.*

Daugherty

Ralph Daugherty

married

Sarah Bollinger Frizel

born to Ralph and Sarah

Samuel Daugherty   George Frederick Daugherty

Berenice Daugherty   Joseph Daugherty

Sarah and Ralph Daugherty

After the death of Joseph Frizel in 1823, Sarah Frizel married Ralph Daugherty on October 13, 1825, with the ceremony performed by Rev. T.P. Green, a Baptist minister. Born to this marriage were Samuel Daugherty, George Frederick Daugherty, Berenice Daugherty, and Joseph Daugherty.

Ralph at one time was a partner in a general store in Jackson with Joseph Russell, who would later marry Mary Frizel, daughter of Sarah and Joseph Frizel. Ralph also served as clerk of the county court and was an Andrew Jackson elector in 1828. Ralph's father William Daugherty, along with his three brothers, had emigrated from Wales and came to Cape Girardeau County by way of Virginia.

Ralph and Sarah's marriage seems to have been filled with problems. One of these resulted from his Catholicism. According to Douglas J. Slawson, of the Congregation of the Mission (C.M.), a feeling of anti-Catholicism arose in the United States during the 1820s, encouraged by the large immigration of Catholics and suspicion of the church's hierarchy. Surprisingly, during this time there was an unusual growth in the Catholic Church in Cape Girardeau and southeast Missouri, which came about with the help of Ralph Daugherty. Slawson has edited and annotated a manuscript published in the *Vincentian Heritage Journal* which details Ralph's involvement.

The writing is entitled *God Is Wonderful in All His Works: A Contemporary Account of Vincentian Activity in the District of Cape Girardeau, Missouri, 1828–1850*, written by John Francis McGerry, C.M., in 1861, describing the role of the Vincentians in the founding of the Catholic religion in this area. The Vincentians are named after their founder, St. Vincent de Paul, and their mission is to follow Jesus Christ, evangelizing the poor. The document, written on forty-four leaves of blue folio paper, was originally stored in the archives of Saint Mary's of the Barrens (which means "prairie") Seminary in Perryville, Missouri, but was relocated to the DeAndreis-Rosati Memorial Archives of the Western Province of the Congregation of the Mission at DePaul University in Chicago, Illinois, in 2001. Related sources include a document called "Pastoral Work of Vincentians at Jackson and Cape Girardeau, 1828–1838," dealing largely with Father John Timon's ministry in the Cape Girardeau area; a manuscript covering work of Fathers John Mary Odin and John Brands with non-Catholics; McGerry's own recollections; letters from the period; the parish registry from St. Vincent de Paul Church in Cape; and Father Timon's recollections, "Barrens Memoir," written in 1861.

McGerry was first assigned as the prefect of Saint Mary's College in Perryville from 1841–1845, continuing in the St. Vincent's College in Cape Girardeau where St. Mary's College was moved in 1843 and the name changed. After a short stay as an assistant pastor in Louisiana, he returned to St. Vincent's in 1847, remaining there until he died in 1873. When McGerry wrote his manuscript, he had been in the Cape Girardeau mission for seventeen years.

The manuscript itself begins in May 1828, with Father John Timon at the Saint Mary's Seminary in Perryville receiving a call from a prisoner under a death sentence and in chains in the Jackson jail. Timon contends that a Baptist minister, Reverend Thomas Parrish Green, along with other Protestants, came to the jail also, and that when Timon began reciting the Apostles' Creed to the prisoner, Timon was accused of exhorting human rather than divine teachings. As a result of the controversy, Timon and Green agreed to a religious debate at the courthouse in Jackson. Green had Mister Greer Davis, a Methodist, as his assistant. According to McGerry, after three hours of discussion, the Protestants were "dumbfounded" and left, with Timon continuing on.

Other debates followed and many people became persuaded to investigate Catholicism for themselves. One of those was Ralph Daugherty. On September 24, 1832, Mr. James Murrian was sent by

Daugherty to the Barrens to ask Father Timon to come to Cape Girardeau that Ralph might be baptized. Timon was delayed for several days, but when he arrived he found that Ralph, because of illness, was at the home of his father, William Daugherty, two miles south on the river. Timon went by boat to William's home and stayed with the family overnight, instructing Ralph and his family in Catholic teachings.

Father Timon baptized Ralph on September 28, 1832, and on September 29, the children of Ralph and Sarah: George Frederick, age six; Samuel, age four; and Berenice, age two. Upon finding that Ralph and his wife Sarah were separated, Timon proceeded to visit Sarah, who was staying at her father's home, to attempt to bring about reconciliation between the two. Although unable to complete that mission, he did succeed in baptizing Joseph Daugherty, the four-month-old son of Ralph and Sarah, who was with his mother. Because of the prejudice toward Catholics, McGerry notes that "when Timon paid visits to the Cape, he had to say Mass 'very privately [at] 6 A.M.' in the Daugherty house" or in a store house.

Although Ralph's wife, Sarah, did not convert to Catholicism, several other family members did. Ralph's sister, Martha Daugherty Abel, was baptized on July 8, 1833, along with her husband Jeremiah Abel, as well as their children, Mary Abel, age eighteen months; Ralph B. Abel, age six, on February 17, 1833; and Sarah Virginia Abel, age three months, on October 24, 1833. The three children of Ralph's other sister, Mary Daugherty Sanford, who was married to Henry Sanford, were also baptized into the church. Pearl, age three, was baptized on February 18, 1833; Theresa, age one month, was baptized on February 13, 1834; and Linus, seventeen months (who would later marry Mattie Russell, the granddaughter of Sarah), was baptized on May 9, 1838. Elizabeth Ramsey Daugherty was baptized shortly after the death of her husband, William, who was baptized on January 31, 1833. Death records show that Elizabeth Ramsey Daugherty was buried from St. Vincent's Church on March 14, 1854, at age eighty-three years. Henry Sanford was buried from the church on November 6, 1861.

In October 1832, Ralph took his three older children to be enrolled in the school at Saint Mary's of the Barrens. Since Sarah had not signed a permission form for the children to attend the school, Ralph was required by the school to sign a release statement that the children's mother could come and visit them, and releasing the school from responsibility if she came to remove them from the school. In

November, Sarah came to the school and persuaded the children to return home with her.

Ralph was very upset that he could not manage the schooling of his children. Although Father Timon tried to calm Ralph by writing letters to him, in January 1833, "his excited mind having brought on phrensy," Ralph attacked his father-in-law's house where his children were living, resulting in Ralph's being wounded and put in jail, where he refused medical care for his wounds. Ralph's brother Evan Daugherty made the forty-mile trip to Perryville to plead with Father Timon to come to the jail. Immediately upon hearing of Ralph's plight, the priest went to the jail and was able to calm Ralph and make him comfortable. After ministering to the other prisoner in the jail, Father Timon returned to Ralph's troubles. Father Timon succeeded in arranging reconciliation between Ralph and George Bollinger, obtained Ralph's release from jail, and was able to get Ralph to consent to leave the area for a while. Before Ralph left, Timon also persuaded Ralph to allow Sarah to have the care of Joseph.

In Ralph's absence, the conflict escalated when two large lawsuits were filed on December 11, 1832, against Ralph: one by George F. Bollinger for $1,540 and the other by the administrator of the estate of Mary Langdon Frizel, deceased mother of Joseph Frizel, for $1,030. The details of the suits are recorded in Cape Girardeau County Circuit Court record book F on page 281. When the lawsuits went to court, the ruling was in favor of the plaintiffs since Ralph was not present for the hearing. In a letter written to Father Timon on December 31, 1832, Ralph's parents, William and Elizabeth Daugherty, expressed their concern that George and his daughter wanted to ruin Ralph both financially and mentally. Ralph wrote of his mental state in a letter to Father Timon, pleading for help, noting his delusions of being a military general, a priest, and a bishop, and his concern that there was to be a division of the church.

Henry Sanford, brother-in-law of Ralph and clerk of the court, hastily went to Saint Mary's to relate to Father Timon what had transpired: Sanford had offered Ralph's property to George Bollinger to cover his claims against Ralph, but his offer was refused by Bollinger. Sanford believed that Bollinger wished to force a public sale of the property which would likely bring a lower amount than the lawsuits required and would give Bollinger a reason to continue to have Ralph arrested.

Sanford made an offer to Rev. Tornatori, the superior at the Barrens, to sell Ralph's property to the seminary for about $2,500.

According to the manuscript, "the gentlemen of the seminary hesitated, thinking it wrong to profit by the misfortune of Daugherty," but promised to purchase the property at a fair price if Ralph could not find a better offer.

On March 28, 1833, Sanford returned to the seminary with Ralph, who was eager to dispose of his property. An agreement was reached for $3,200, with the Vincentians acquiring five pieces of property:

> two town lots in Cape Girardeau, the Decatur lot (forty-five and a half acres) just outside of town [where the seminary would be built], the swamp farm (179 acres) about a mile and a half below the site of the college, and another piece of land (158 acres) in Scott County. . . . Daugherty received $2,500 in cash and agreed to leave undisturbed (for the education of his children) . . . the balance of seven hundred dollars and the amount of sale of some [live]stock and other articles.

The seminary was able to make the purchase due to a loan of $2,000 made to the seminary from John Casey of Potosi. This transaction was recorded on March 28, 1833, and can be found in Book H, pages 117–118.

Since Ralph's father was living at the swamp farm that was sold in the deal, he now had no place to live, but the seminary agreed to permit him to remain for a time without rent.

Timon gives the following summary of the transaction:

> To save him [Ralph Daugherty] from losing his property under the unscrupulous persecution, it was necessary to purchase that property from him. It is the most beautiful property in the country. The Seminary [Saint Vincent's College, built in 1843], with its noble and spacious grounds; and the beautiful Church of St. Vincent [built in 1852] stand on part of it.

The seminary buildings and grounds were closed in 1979 and later sold to Southeast Missouri State University. The land that was once the property of Ralph Daugherty became the River Campus of the university in the fall of 2007.

On June 23, 1833, at a time when an epidemic of cholera was raging in Cape Girardeau County, which in the end caused 128 deaths, Father Timon was called to the swamp farm south of Cape Girardeau to see Ralph, who was very ill. Timon first heard the confessions of both Ralph and his father, and then rushed back to Jackson to minister to another family, arriving there in the dark. Having been informed that William Daugherty had died, he once again traveled the nine miles back to the swamp farm not only in the dark but also in the rain that had begun. He found William Daugherty's corpse in the bed

St. Vincent's Seminary, Cape Girardeau, 1890. *Photo courtesy of Ron Kirby.*

where he had expired, surrounded by family and friends sleeping on the floor. After offering a prayer, Father Timon was given a place to sleep on the only bed in the house. The corpse was moved over to the wall, a clean sheet spread over the body, whereupon Timon shared the bed with William's lifeless body and slept soundly.

On September 19, 1834, George Frederick Bollinger was appointed by the court as guardian of George F. Daugherty, Samuel Daugherty, Berenice Daugherty, and Joseph Daugherty, minor children of Ralph Daugherty.

Ralph once again began having mental disturbances and made claims to the seminary for the livestock, which had been sold, and the $700 still on deposit for the children's schooling, which had not been used. Over a period of three years, Ralph was allowed to draw out the $700 plus about $100 more. But in 1838, he found himself penniless. Ralph died in 1850 and is buried in the Bollinger cemetery in Burfordville.

According to family stories, Ralph was an abusive husband. Sarah's father George Frederick Bollinger used his influence as president pro-tem of the Missouri State Senate to secure a quiet divorce for Sarah, which was kept from public knowledge for many years. In the Vandivort history, Harriet Smith states that she has all the court records of domestic violence that Sarah brought against Ralph. These detail how Sarah's father was able to use his influence and money to keep Ralph from influencing his children or deeding George's property to the Jesuits as Ralph wished to do.

Slawson in a footnote adds:

> Vincentian difficulties with the Daugherty family did not end here. In 1872 George Frederick Daugherty, Ralph's oldest son, sued Saint Vincent's College for the property sold to the Vincentians by his father. George claimed that Tornatore and Timon had taken advantage of Ralph's insanity in order 'to cheat, injure, and defraud' him and his heirs out of their rightful property 'by fraud, religious fervor, fear, and divers other fraudulent practices.' George also alleged that in 1833 the property was worth, not $3,200, but $15,000. He claimed further that, even though the Vincentians had agreed to pay $3,200, no money ever changed hands. . . . Daugherty lost the suit.

An interesting side note: After writing this section, I discovered upon rereading the abstract of the Range C Lots 8 and 9, upon which our house sits, that on January 19, 1826, Ralph Daugherty, "being the highest and best bidder," purchased Lot 9 for the sum of $19.50. The property had been foreclosed on a complaint by Greer W. Davis against Doctor Jonas N. Menefee, who formerly had a medical shop in the white house on the lot. The abstract does not show when Ralph's ownership ended.

The 1850 census shows that Sarah is once more a widow. Living with her were her daughter, Sarah Josephine Frizel, age twenty-seven, and her son, George F. Daugherty, age twenty-four. According to the *Southern Advocate* newspaper, Joseph Daugherty, youngest son of Sarah and Ralph, died at the home of his grandfather, Col. George Bollinger, in Whitewater, November 10, 1838. He was six years of age. After the death of her father, Sarah became the owner of Bollinger Mill and, along with her two sons George Frederick and Samuel, operated the mill until the advent of the Civil War.

Sarah Bollinger Frizel Daugherty. *Photo courtesy of Jackson Heritage Association.*

52

The Russells of St. Louis:

James and Lucy Russell

Russell

James Russell

Married

Elizabeth O'Bannon

Born to James and Elizabeth

Joseph William Russell   Martha Jane Russell

Mary Frizel, middle daughter of Sarah and Joseph Frizel, married Joseph W. Russell on November 9, 1843, in Jackson, Missouri. When I followed the recommendation of Susan Rehkopf, the archivist at the Episcopal Diocese of Missouri, to read *The Old Gravois Coal Diggings* by Mary Joan Boyer, I discovered that Joseph's uncles, William Russell and Joseph Russell, had come west in 1805 from Virginia by way of East Tennessee and Illinois, "seeking their fortune." In St. Louis William stopped and made a purchase of 432 acres in west St. Louis, bordered on the north by Arsenal Street, on the east by Grand, on the west by Kingshighway, and on the south by Gravois. Arsenal Street is located just south of what is presently Tower Grove Park. Part of the land was later used for the 1904 World's Fair, but in 1805, early settlers of St. Louis were faced with swamp land which was plagued with mosquitoes, malaria, and other fevers, as well as Indian hostilities. Joseph left William in St. Louis, going south where he purchased property at Bird's Point, Missouri.

James W. Russell, the brother of William and Joseph Russell and father of Joseph W. Russell, was born February 27, 1786, in Rockridge County, Virginia, to Joseph Russell and Margaret Campbell

Russell. After fighting in the War of 1812, James later migrated with his family to East Tennessee, where he left them and moved on to the Missouri territory. On his arrival in Missouri, he first settled in Jackson, where he was a newspaper editor and proprietor of the Eagle Hotel. There he met Elizabeth O'Bannon, who was from Cape Girardeau County. They were married in 1815 in Hardy County, Virginia, becoming the parents of Joseph William Russell, born November 1, 1819; and Martha Jane Russell, born April 28, 1817.

Russell

James Russell

Married

Lucy Bent

Born to James and Lucy

Charles S. Russell   Russella Lucy Russell

About 1811, James purchased from his brother, William, the estate in St. Louis, which he developed into a beautiful plantation with fine orchards, vineyards, flower and vegetable gardens, and pastures with cattle. After the death of his wife in 1825, James moved to St. Louis, where he married Lucy Bent, who was twenty years younger than he.

A homestead was built at the intersection of the present streets of Wyoming and Oak Hill, so named due to the abundance of oak trees. After a few years passed and the pioneer urge returned, James had agreed to sell the plantation and move on to a new location. However, he took one more stroll through the plantation to consider his decision and happened upon a gulley which had been washed by a recent rain. Shining in the side of the gulley was a dark seam which turned out to be coal. He reneged on his promise to sell the property and instead, about 1820, opened up a coal mine which supplied the city of St. Louis with coal for the next seventy years. The coal deposit, near the intersection of Tholozan and Morganford, was known locally as the Old Gravois Coal Diggings, shortened to "The Diggins." In 1855, a superb clay which had superior fireproof qualities was found on the property; soon, in addition to the Russell Coal Mines, there was the Oak Hill Fire Clay Works, making fine quality bricks.

James served as a judge of the St. Louis County Court and in the Missouri state legislature. He died in 1850, leaving a wealthy estate to his wife and children. Some of this estate would be passed to the descendants of his son Joseph, including Julia Russell Harris. His widow Lucy was very philanthropic, leaving in her will property deeded to several churches in the estate she owned, one being the Holy Innocents Episcopal Church founded by several members of the Russell family. Two of the local streets, Lucy and Bent, are named for Lucy.

In a letter written from Crystal Springs to his brother Joseph in 1849, William reported on the cholera outbreak in St. Louis.

> James, his wife and two daughters, are recovering from cholera. Seven of the negroes on the plantation died of cholera, the rest of them are recovering. All on James' plantation had the cholera. At Crystal Springs there is only myself and ten or twelve slaves—as yet no case of cholera or any other sickness here, though sickness and death have been most awful all around us, on every side. The cholera is abating but still exists both in St. Louis and county—it spread nearly everywhere. The newspapers have not told near the whole of it. In this city no less than three or four thousand have died in the last three months, and at least twenty or thirty thousand have fled to other parts. The streets are thinned of the moving crowds to be seen when you were here. The season of bilious and bowel complaints is approaching and following the cholera, may well be dreaded. Too feeble and tired to write more now. Remaining your respectful brother. William Russell.

Born to James and Lucy Russell were Charles S. Russell and Russella Lucy Russell. Charles's son, Charles M. Russell, became a famous cowboy artist. As a young boy he wanted nothing to do with regular school work, but was obsessed with art, even carving his mother's soap and potatoes into images, and drawing animals. He rode his pony through the coal diggings, startling the workers with his wild riding and war whoops. One of his favorite places to ride was through the lawns of Henry Shaw's Gardens. His dream was to go west, see the sights he dreamed of, and practice his artistic talents. Finally relenting, his parents allowed him to go to Montana at age sixteen, thinking that once he saw the actual hardships in the real West, he would come quickly home. However, an old hunter named Jake Hoover befriended Charles and encouraged him in his art. Charles had found the life he dreamed of.

Today thousands of visitors each year view his world-famous paintings and sculptures of cowboys and Indians in the museum that sits beside his house and log cabin studio in Great Falls, Montana.

The Russells of Jackson:

Mary and Joseph Russell

Russell

Joseph William Russell

married

Mary Langdon Frizel

Born to Joseph and Mary

Martha Jane Russell   Julia Elizabeth Russell

James William Russell

Mary Langdon Frizel, who would become the mother of Julia Russell, followed her mother's example and, at the age of thirteen, traveled by stagecoach to Bethlehem, Pennsylvania, to the Moravian Seminary for Girls. She continued to be interested in learning all her life and left a large list of books in her will to be shared with her three children. According to Mary's obituary, which appeared in the *Cape Girardeau Democrat* on September 14, 1895, Mary spent one hour each day reading classical literature.

Mary and Joseph Russell had three children born to them: Martha Jane Russell, known as Mattie, born July 22, 1846; Julia Elizabeth Russell, born October 10, 1848; and James William Russell, born July 7, 1851. Joseph became a partner in a mercantile store in Jackson with Ralph Daugherty and later with Charles Welling, the husband of Mary Russell's sister Elizabeth. Joseph, who was born November 1, 1819, in Mason County, Kentucky, was an enterprising man, using his skills as a civil engineer to survey the railroads in

Illinois. He accumulated a huge estate with farms in southern Illinois; 640 acres at Bird's Point, Missouri; and real estate in St. Louis inherited from his father. He owned several lots in Cape Girardeau, including Lot 8, Range C which became 313 Themis Street. In the probate file for Joseph, I found the original bill of sale that he had signed in 1850 to purchase the lot. The 1851 Cape Girardeau County property tax record shows that Joseph had land valued at $1,500, seventeen slaves valued at $4,500, six horses/$150, six cattle/$35, two clocks/watches $25, one share stock/$75, and one poll/$12.94. A parcel of land of 141½ acres was leased from Stephen Byrd, in addition to 200 acres on the farm where Joseph was residing, leased from Lewellyn Russell.

Joseph Russell was in St. Louis for business purposes when he became ill with cholera, which was rampant in the city. A family story tells that when he returned home and passed away from the illness, his personal slave was so distraught that he lay down on Joseph's bed, also becoming ill from the cholera and dying.

Since Joseph died without a will, settling his estate was quite involved. His probate folder at the Cape Girardeau County Archives contains a lengthy list of the inventory of the mercantile store he co-owned with his brother-in-law Charles Welling. Also, a list of people with unpaid account balances contains some rather amusing reasons why the bills are outstanding. Charles Welling has written such remarks as "worthless," "dead, insolvent," "of Bollinger County, worthless," "dead—sent to Wayne County for allowance and never could hear more of it," "absconded," "left for parts unknown," "refused to pay—had paid it in meal," "sent to penitentiary—worthless." Also in the folder is the bill for ten dollars paid to Cornelius Slack, the maker of Joseph's coffin.

A sale bill of slaves belonging to the estate of Joseph W. Russell listed the following:

Name of slave	Purchaser	Amount
Richard	N. W. Watkins	$826
Henry	William Johnson	$501
Washington	Bernard S. McGuire	$952.50
		$2279.50

Dr. Cannon V. McFarland presented a bill to Col. H.H.M. Williams, the administrator of the J.W. Russell estate, for the services administered to the slaves owned by Joseph for a total of $11.87. Services included:

an Emeter and a cath to boy Frank	$1.37
2 visits and dressing Negro child's leg	$1.50
2 visits to Tom and meds	$1.50
To attend to Tom and child	$1.50
To attendance & meds to Tom 2 days	$2.50
To do as same	$2.50
To a visit and meds	$1.00

There was also a sale beginning on September 16, 1852, lasting for four days, of the personal property of Joseph in order to pay the bills remaining in his estate. An amazingly long list included bonnets, thimbles, thread, a sleigh, cows, horses, tools, fabric, china, shawls, and furniture. Mary Russell bought a cow for $13.30 and a plow for $4. Some other items that sold were empty sacks $1.69, vinegar $2.50, laudanum (a pain killer derived from opium) 10 cents, cinnamon 20 cents, ribbons 10 cents, asafetida 25 cents, six hogs $15.05, spectacles 12 cents, and one sow and pigs $2.00. The sale total was $1,146.92.

Mary was only thirty-one years of age when Joseph died on June 21, 1852, leaving her with Mattie, six, Julia, three, and James, one. She never remarried. Trust funds were set up for the three children with George W. Parker, T. Gustine Russell, and Charles S. Russell serving as trustees.

Mary's obituary appeared in the *Cape Girardeau Democrat* on September 14, 1895, as follows:

DEATH CALLS
And Mrs. Mary L. Russell is no More
    She Lived the Life of a Christian and Met Death Without Fear.
    Entered into rest on September 10th, 1895. Mrs. Mary L. Russell, aged 73 years.
    In her death there departed from among us a woman of pure heart and capacious intellect. To friends no one could have been more loyal than she was to hers, or, in an hour of perplexity a wiser counselor. From infancy to advanced age, as daughter, wife, mother and neighbor she discharged every duty. No acrid speech or bitter reproach ever escaped her lips or found lodge-

ment in her bosom. Her toleration and charity were as wide extended as humanity. Every ill of life that befell her was met undauntedly, and whatever else was the result she emerged a truer and a more Christian woman. She had much of which to be proud. She had an ancestry which, on the paternal side, for generations was justly distinguished for culture and successful management of great affairs. Her father, Joseph Frizzell [*sic*], was of French descent, though his place of nativity was New Hampshire. He was educated, and for many years resided in Boston: he afterwards moved West and was a successful merchant in St. Louis and Jackson. He was master of several languages, and spoke them fluently without perceptible accent. His business letters now in possession of his family show them to be the production of an alert and cultivated business man, and deserve publication. He died at an early age but left a handsome provision for his family.

Mrs. Russell's mother [Sarah Bollinger Frizel Daugherty] was a woman of large mental endowments and received an education bestowed upon but few young women in America in the first years of this century, and was gifted with a remarkable talent for painting. She was educated at Salem, North Carolina, at which point, at one time was located the most celebrated female school in this country.

Mary L. Frizzell was born July 28th, 1822, and in her early childhood was baptized by the Rev. Benjamin Harroll, the first Episcopal minister who found his way into Missouri, and through all her life was a devoted member of that church. In her early girlhood she was sent to a female school at Bethel, Penn. to be educated, where she remained until she was graduated, and where she imbibed a love for literature, which remained with her and which love she indulged far into the period of her last long fatal illness. Through all her life it was her rule not to permit herself to become so absorbed with her social or domestic duties, but that she could devote at least an hour each day to classic literature. In her maidenhood she was largely under the tutilage of her maternal grand-father, Col. Geo. Frederick Bollinger, a man conspicuous for ardent patriotism, great force of character, originality and success in his interprises, and to him his grand-child was indebted for much of her worldly wisdom. In 1843 she was married to Joseph W. Russell of St. Louis, who was a civil engineer by profession, a man of many accomplishments, and was a member of a family whose social position was equal to that of any, a distinction transmitted through many generations.

Their married life was of but a few years duration, it was severed by the untimely death of the husband in 1852, an event which she never ceased to mourn through 43 years of widowhood. She was a proud woman, that pride which is born of distinguished ancestry, of conscious worth and a knowledge that every duty in life is well done: it was that noble pride that save the true woman from vulgar ostentation. From death she had nothing to fear, like the faithful servant she could say: "Master, thou deliveredst to me five talents: behold, I have gained beside them, five talents more."

Mrs. Russell leaves, besides many friends, three children to mourn her departure. Mrs. Martha Sanford, wife of Hon. Linus Sanford, of Jackson, Missouri, Mrs. Julia E. Harris, wife of Dr. S. S. Harris, of Cape Girardeau, Missouri, and Dr. James W. Russell of Birds Point, Missouri.

Mary left an extensive inheritance to her heirs. First was the property. For her daughter Mattie, she left her "house and lot, and my lots adjacent thereto in the same block or square in which said house is, all located in the city of Jackson." To her daughter Julia, "My lot and house thereon, now partly occupied by James McKenna, and fronting on the Levee [on the water front of the Mississippi River], in Range D in the city of Cape Girardeau, Mo." For her son James, "My farm in Mississippi County, Missouri, near the town of Birds Point, and near the Mississippi River, being the same farm I acquired by virtue of partition deeds among the heirs of my deceased husband." Both daughters received their property as the will stated "for her sole and separate use, and free from any claim control and interest thereof and therein of her husband." To her grandson Linus Sanford Jr., she devised the undivided one-half of the ninety-six acres of the farm located in what is called "the Bend," north of and near the City of Cape Girardeau. Possibly the large curve of the river there was the source of the name of the area as well as the name "Big Bend Road." The farm had been acquired by partition deeds among the heirs of Joseph Russell and partly from the Sampy heirs.

She left one-fourth of her St. Louis lots to her grandchildren Linus, Mattie, and Julia Sanford, children of Mattie Sanford, and to Lizzie and Annie Russell, children of James Russell, property which would be managed by Mary's trustees. The other three-fourths of the St. Louis property would be devised to Mary's children, Mattie, Julia, and James, share and share alike, as would the lots in the town of Bird's Point, Mississippi County, Missouri. Ten shares of Capital Stock of the First National Bank at par value of $100 would be set aside for the grandchildren, also to be held in trust. As in all bequests in her will, she stipulates that in the case of female heirs the inheritance is "for her sole and separate use."

Mary's farm on Crooked Creek near White Water Station in Cape Girardeau County, which comprised about 106 acres and was inherited partly from her father Joseph Frizel and partly from the heirs of Frizel and Ranney, was to be held in trust and managed by her trustees until the youngest grandchild reached majority, and then the property would belong to her three children, share and share alike.

Mary also willed to Mary Amanda Blomeyer, the daughter of Mary's son-in-law, Dr. S.S. Harris, and his first wife, five shares of the Capital Stock of The First National Bank of Cape Girardeau of the par value of $100.

Finally, we have the family heirlooms bequeathed to her children. To Martha, Mary left "one old family silver mug, one half of my jewelry and all the furniture I now own and now being in the Sandford [sic] house in Jackson, Mo., and also one-half of all my bedding and bed clothes, not otherwise bequeathed." To Julia she bequeathed "one old family silver porringer [a small bowl for eating porridge], fork and spoon, all the furniture I now own in her house in Cape Girardeau . . . one half of my jewelry, and also one half of all my bedding and bed clothes not otherwise bequeathed." To her son James she gave her "old family Bible, with clasp of which is the name of 'Pemberton.' Also a feather bed pillow and bolster now at the house of Julia E. Harris. To my granddaughter, Julia Sandford [sic] my secretary." And as pointed out earlier, her books were to be divided equally among her three children.

Mary's closing paragraph expresses her wishes to her daughter, Julia:

> I request, that if my daughter Julia E. Harris shall not need or use any or all of the property given her in this will and that some thereof remain at her death, that she will and give said remaining part to my grandchildren then living or their bodily heirs: But, the words used in this item shall under no

circumstances and in no event be construed by any person or any Court of Law, Equity or Probate, to alter change limit or in anywise effect the property given her by this will shall be construed as if this item had not been written; it being merely intended to express my wishes, leaving my daughter to freely act as she pleases.

Mary appointed her children Martha, Julia, and James as trustees to carry out the mandates of her will.

Mary was devoted to the Episcopalian faith for more than forty years. In her probate file was a receipt paying her pledge of $48 to support the minister and $2.25 for missions. In her will under Item II she states, "I will my soul to God, who gave it, trusting in His infinite mercy for forgiveness of sins and believing in a joyful resurrection in the life to come, I desire that my body be interred in Christian burial in the Jackson Mo. Cemetery by the side of my husband." She also willed "to the Right Reverend Daniel S. Tuttle D. D., Bishop of Missouri of the Protestant Episcopal Church, and his successors in office, in trust, the following real estate: A lot of ground in the City of Jackson, Missouri, known as the 'Garden Lot' and being opposite to and across the street from the real estate devised to Martha J. Sandford [sic] in item two." The property is located at 206 East Washington Street. The condition attached to the gift was that a house of worship or church should be built on the property within twenty-five years from the date of her death (1895); if this requirement was not met, the real estate should pass to her lawful heirs.

The Episcopal Diocese of Missouri was organized in St. Louis in 1840, but an established church was not founded in Cape Girardeau County until 1876 when a missionary, Rev. George Moore, came, holding services in Cape Girardeau in Common Pleas Courthouse while the church was being built on the corner of Themis and Fountain. The church held several types of fund raisers such as minstrel shows, teas, concessions at the Opera House, and even solicitations of funds in the local saloons, in addition to pledges by the members. The new church was completed on September 18, 1878.

In the meantime, according to Susan Rehkopf, an archivist with the Episcopal Diocese in St. Louis, a mission known as St. John's Church began life in 1872 in Jackson as an unorganized mission with the following officers: Julia Russell serving as treasurer; Mr. Thomas Struthers, warden; and Mr. C.P. Fulenwider, clerk. Official services began October 1, 1876. The mission shared clergy with the Cape Girardeau church. A note in *The Church News*, a newspaper of the St. Louis Diocese, tells about the work going on in Jackson in January 1872.

> The Rev. Edwin Wickens, of S. Luke's Hospital, has been on a visit to Jackson, Missouri. On the last Sunday of the old year, he held service in the morning in the house of Mrs. Russell [Mary Russell], and at night in the Baptist Church, and also on the Monday and Tuesday nights following in the same place. Good congregations were present at all services.

On July 29, 1903, a petition was sent to Rev. Tuttle in St. Louis stating thus:

> The undersigned respectfully represent that they have associated themselves together as a Mission of the Protestant Episcopal Church of this Diocese. They hereby declare their adhesion to the doctrine, discipline, and form of worship of said church, and to their submission to the ecclesiastical authority of the Diocese of Missouri and the causes thereof. They therefore pray that they may be organized as a Mission.
> Dated the 29th day of July, 1903
> Leslie Fenton Potter Priest-in-charge

The other founding members were Martha Peterman and Julia Adele Sanford (daughters of Mattie and Linus Sanford); Martha Jane "Mattie" Russell Sanford; Linus Sanford; Margaret, Kate G., and Nadine Fulenwider; Laura A., Katherine, and Ed Frazier; A.M., M.E., Daisy, and Gertrude Morgan; Norman D. Blue; Kate Dennis; Rita O. Limbaugh; T.D. Hamlin; Constance Peterman; and Mrs. L.G. Todd.

A lengthy article about the Jackson mission appeared in the September 1903 issue of *The Church News*.

JACKSON
Proposition for a Church Building
   The Rev. Mr. Patton, who has been giving services in Jackson, issues the following appeal on behalf of the congregation.
   Jackson is the county-seat of Cape Girardeau County, and a place of 1,700 inhabitants. The Bishop has made annual visi-

tations there for a number of years. A devoted church woman left lots on condition that a church be erected within a given number of years after her death. The lots are splendid for the purpose and are most desirably located.

Regular monthly services were begun by the undersigned in December, 1902. The people have succeeded in raising $800 toward a church. At least $1500 will be needed. Will you generously come to our aid? Any amount from fifty cents up will be gratefully appreciated and acknowledged.
Faithfully Yours in Christ,
Leslie Fenton Potter
Dean of the Southern Convocation

A further note was written by Rev. Tuttle seeking pledges for contributions to the project.

> The people of our Church at Jackson are very earnest and faithful for any help given to them in building their church.
> Daniel S. Tuttle
> Bishop of Missouri
> Kindly mail the following to Rev. L.F. Potter, Kirkwood Station, St. Louis, Missouri.
> Upon receiving this statement countersigned by the Bishop as a guarantee that $1500 has been raised, I will send to Mr. Linus Sanford, Treasurer, Jackson, Missouri, $_____toward building a church for the Mission of the Redeemer.
> Signed_____

On September 18, 1903, the mission officially became the Church of the Redeemer. *The Church News,* November 1904, reports:

> In the absence of the bishop, Dean Potter laid the corner stone for the Church of the Redeemer, on St. Michael and All Angels' Day. The church is to be a neat and substantial brick building of Gothic architecture. When completed, it will seat about 140 persons. It is to be heated by a furnace, and will have convenient rooms on either side of the chancel for sacristy and vestry. Complete, it will cost about $2000. The building is already enclosed and the contractor reports that he will be ready to turn it over to the committee November 30th.

The church was constructed on the property willed to the Diocese by Mary Frizel, and with the cornerstone being laid on September 29, 1904, Joseph Frizel and his daughter Mary's dream of an Episcopal church in the area had been realized.

However, the congregation never experienced significant growth, the final blow being the spring storm of 1923 which badly damaged the building. The April 1923 issue of *The Church News* reports on the storm:

> About eight o'clock on the evening of Sunday, March 11, a cyclone swept through this town, doing much damage to stores and residences. Three churches were seriously injured, among them our little Chapel. The building was bent right in the middle, the center of the south wall leaning in and the north wall out. All the shingles were stripped from one side of roof, and some of the bricks torn off of one corner. Repairing would mean practical rebuilding, which is out of the question inasmuch as only three communicants live in the town. It was a very attractive, very churchly little building, and its loss is bemoaned especially by Mrs. Linus Sanford, who for many years had a thriving Sunday School in this mission. Through her efforts this little mission has reared and sent elsewhere a number of devoted communicants of the Church. In recent years, constant removals scattered the small congregation.

In 1924, the Vestry of Christ Church requested and was granted permission from the diocese to sell the property to First Presbyterian Church in Jackson.

The large walnut altar in the chapel was made by a Swiss carver and had been displayed at the 1904 World's Fair. It apparently was bought there by Julia Adele Sanford (granddaughter of Mary) and Clyde A. Vandivort while on their honeymoon. Featured on the altar were inlaid hand-carved medallions symbolizing the four gospels. After the church was closed, the altar was moved to the Sanford home where family services could be held. In 1926, Mrs. Linus Sanford gave the altar to Christ Episcopal Church in Cape Girardeau where it was used until February 1976, when the chancel was renovated. The medallions were removed from the old altar and incorporated into the newly designed altar.

There are two conflicting stories about the history of the altar. One story says the altar was purchased by Julia Harris at the fair

Charles Welling. *Courtesy of Jackson Heritage Association.*

and given to the Jackson mission. However, she died in February 1903 and the fair was not held until April 30, 1904–December 1, 1904. A family member says that Julia and Clyde Vandivort bought the altar at the World's Fair when they were there on their honeymoon but gave it to Christ Episcopal Church. However, church records show members of the family (seven children of the Vandivorts) being baptized into the Church of the Redeemer in Jackson over the period of time it was in existence between 1904 and 1924. It would seem that the altar was purchased by the Vandivorts and donated to the Church of the Redeemer and only later donated by Mrs. Sanford to Christ Episcopal Church in Cape Girardeau after there was no longer a church or mission in Jackson.

The First Presbyterian Church, Jackson, which bought the property, had been organized at the home of Elizabeth and Charles Welling on May 15, 1864. Mrs. Sarah Bollinger Frizel Daugherty and Charles Welling were founding members of the church. Welling was elected the Ruling Elder and served for thirty-five years, being the sole elder for twenty-three of those years. He is considered the father of that church. The new church was dedicated in 1940.

The Williamses of Jackson:

Berenice and Harrison Harvey Minton Williams

Williams

Harrison Harvey Minton Williams

married

Berenice Daugherty

Born to Harrison and Berenice

Samuel Daugherty Williams

George Williams

Joseph Welling Williams

Russell H. Williams

Minnie B. Williams

Charles Frederick Williams

Sarah Conway Williams

Clara E. Williams

Harrison Williams

Big Hill Farm

When Berenice Daugherty, the daughter of Ralph and Sarah Bollinger Daugherty, was seventeen, she married Harrison Harvey Minton Williams on January 21, 1847, at the home of Berenice's mother. The couple made their home on Big Hill Farm, which originally belonged to Berenice's paternal grandfather, William Daugherty, who named the farm. Berenice preferred the name "Fairy Lawn." The farm, located near Jackson in Cape Girardeau County, was obtained by William through a Spanish land grant in 1799, in appreciation for his serving as a captain in Houck's Spanish Regiment, as well as serving on the local Legislative Council. In 1806,

The Williams "I-house" on Big Hill Farm, built in the 1850s. *Photo by author.*

when the Spanish land grants were questioned after the Louisiana Purchase, William's grant was confirmed in a document signed by John Adams. Information about the farm is detailed in the Big Hill Farmstead Historic District National Register of Historic Places Report, the farm having been placed on the register December 22, 1999.

Ralph Daugherty inherited the farm from his father William and sold it to George Frederick Bollinger in 1830. George's daughter Sarah inherited his estate upon George's death in 1842. Included in the estate was a trust fund for Berenice: 337 acres of land, including all of the Big Hill Farm, which she received in 1849 after her marriage. In the 1850 census, the Williamses were living at Big Hill in the old Daugherty home, which is no longer standing.

According to the well-kept diary of Harrison Williams, the building of the new farmhouse was begun in the early 1850s. On February 1, 1854, Williams wrote: "Last month spent principally in cutting and splitting Brick wood," probably referring to wood that would be used in the kiln to make bricks for the house. King and Frank, most likely slaves, dug the foundation, with the clay from the excavation being used to make bricks. An entry dated December 31, 1854, states: "Besides ordinary farm work, quarried rock, made brick & put up walls of house–crops poor." The entry on July 3, 1855, noted the conclusion of the construction: "Moved into new Brick House, Finished Barn."

The house is a brick I-House with a central passage and a veranda across the front of the house. The I-House style, so called because this type of architecture was so dominant in Indiana, Illinois, and Iowa (all states beginning with an I), was brought to America from Britain in the colonial period and features a house that is two stories high, two rooms wide, and one room deep. It was also a very popular house style in Missouri during that time period. The Big Hill house has a two-story "ell" in the back. The Williams house contains elements of both Greek Revival and Italian styling, such as latticework and bracketed eaves on the veranda. Also still on the farm are three outbuildings: an 1850s timber frame barn, an 1850s cabin/workshop, and an 1870s wagon shed. Berenice attended Mrs. Guild's school in Philadelphia, and it has been suggested that perhaps she found some of her ideas for the new house when she traveled in the eastern United States. On July 4, 1855, the new home was completed and the family combined a Fourth of July celebration with a housewarming.

Williams received his law education in Maryland and, upon returning to Cape Girardeau County, read law in the office of Col. Thomas Ranney, being admitted to the Missouri Bar in 1842 at the age of twenty-one. However, two years after his marriage to Berenice, when she inherited Big Hill Farmstead, he became a very diligent farmer. From 1849 to 1858, he kept a meticulous diary documenting every aspect of farming in that time period. Under his leadership, the farm's cultivable land increased greatly, from ninety acres in 1850 to two hundred acres in 1860, and crop yields nearly doubled. Williams also took advantage of the mechanized farm equipment available. He noted the planting of Zimmerrian wheat with a Pennock patented drill that "works finely." His diary records purchases of a deep tiller plow, a McCormick mower and reaper, and a jumping shovel plow.

This last implement was a most unusual one. Although Williams left us no comments on his or his workers' experiences with the "jumpin' shovel plow," the tool received quite a review in the *Pittsburg Gazette Times* of June 2, 1912. Described there as "The Jumpin' Shovel Plow: An Implement That Drove Boys to Cities," the plow was much heavier than the usual plow, with a long, blade-edged iron bar called a cutter in front of the shovel. When the cutter struck a root it was unable to cut, the plough jumped out of the ground like a "hungry trout rising to a fat fly." When the plow came up, its handles could break the ribs of the plowboy. The horses would then join in the fray, giving a yank to the plow and "seem[ing] to think his ribs were a xylophone."

Any previously unbroken ribs would surely be broken this time. According to the story, "If you made the shovel hit the earth every 10 feet you were inclined to brag about plowing. . . . In the 'new ground' not previously plowed you were supposed to be tearing up the ground but instead most of the time, the plow was either going to the tree tops, hitting a rib or shoulder on the way up, or coming down and landing on you if you didn't dodge."

Williams's diary also records experimentation with seeds in which Williams planted twelve acres of corn using seed which had been soaked in potassium nitrate. He then planted untreated seed in another part of the field. He also tried different varieties of wheat and planting times in fall and winter. However, he failed to notate the results of his efforts.

According to Williams's diary, farm owners cooperated at harvesting time, moving from farm to farm with their workers and equipment. In July 1850, Williams noted that his hands helped D. Green thrashing wheat, and later, on August 2, it was his turn with thirteen hands including his plus "a driver and feeder, 3 hired but 3 exchanges." An entry dated the next day indicated, "Quit today at dinner—over half done." An August 8 entry mentioned helping E. Criddle thrash wheat, "very hot." On August 13, his crew was thrashing wheat at the Russells' farm (probably his brother-in-law Joseph W. Russell).

A note in the diary on March 8, 1853, states: "Mrs. Russell's Frank came down last evening and set in to work by the year today. I am to pay what I think I can afford, say $20 more or less." By this time Mary Russell had become a widow.

The bumper crops included corn, rye, wheat, oats, and timothy. The cellar was bountifully filled with pumpkins, sweet potatoes, squash, and apples. Other products from the farm included honey, beeswax, maple syrup, butter, and wool. Livestock on the farm included hogs, sheep, and cattle. Williams's diary records on February 1, 1854, "Put up 3367 lbs pork this winter. Sold 927 lbs. Total 4294 lbs. Slaughtered 27 hogs." So Williams had expanded the farm not only to provide for his family and farm hands, slave or free, but also to have extra for a cash market.

The Williams family faced challenges during the Civil War as did all the other residents of Cape Girardeau County. Williams was opposed to secession although census records show that he owned six slaves in 1850 and nine slaves in 1860, along with two slave houses. The Daughertys were strong abolitionists and pro-Union, but the

Bollingers were pro-South. Big Hill escaped damage to the property during the war, perhaps due to the fact that two Union soldiers were residing there in 1863 and 1864. After Lincoln issued the Emancipation Proclamation, Williams freed his slaves, but some of them remained on the farm as paid workers.

A slave by the name of Barley made the trips by wagon to take grain to the Bollinger Mill to be ground into flour and corn meal. He also made shoes for the children, dug family graves, and played the violin. After he was freed, he still returned to visit the family and to play duets with the piano, an 1847 Chickering that was a gift to Berenice on her seventeenth birthday.

Williams's interests extended beyond farming. On February 28, 1851, the General Assembly of the Missouri legislature incorporated the Cape Girardeau McAdamizing and Plank Road Company. The company was authorized to build a road from Cape Girardeau to Jackson and on to Bollinger's Mill, which was used through the early years of the twentieth century. The last leg to Mine LaMotte in Madison County was never completed. Williams was the president of the company in 1852. He was also involved in other civic activities such as chairing a committee to attract a railroad, finding a site for a normal school, and organizing the Jackson Public School System, serving as president of the school board in 1874.

Berenice found the post-war years especially difficult since she had been accustomed to having five female slaves to help out with the housework. In 1868, in writing to her son Samuel, who was away at the Kentucky Military Institute, she complained about "being in grease all day at hog-killing time." In 1870, she "wanted to go off to some new country where she could live a different and better life." In the census of that year, Berenice's rather large household consisted of H.H.M. Williams, age forty-eight; Berenice, forty; Samuel, eighteen; Minnie, twelve; George, ten; Joseph, six; Harrison, five; Sarah Daugherty, sixty-nine; Sarah Frizel, forty-seven; Peterson, twenty-four, farmhand; and Lorena Daugherty, nineteen, black housekeeper. In 1872, Berenice was "disgusted with farm life, milking cows [eight of them], carrying out slops, feeding pigs is not what I fancy," she explained in another letter to her son.

After the war when farm workers were scarce and the economy was suffering, Williams's interest in farming seemed to wane, and he began to spend more time in Jackson on his legal practice and his mercantile store, which operated on the southeast corner of Main and South High Streets for more than forty years. A tenant farmer

H.H.M. and Berenice Williams. *Photos courtesy of Jackson Heritage Association.*

was hired to run the farm. After Berenice's death in 1875, Williams moved to Jackson. A note in *Clyde Arthur and Julia Sanford Vandivort of Cape Girardeau, Missouri, Their Ancestors and Descendants* indicates that after Berenice's death, Sarah Daugherty, now age seventy-four, stayed on with the Williams family to help with the rearing of the children who were left: Minnie, seventeen; George, fifteen; Joseph, eleven; and Harrison, ten.

The Williamses' son Samuel returned to Jackson after attending Washington University in St. Louis to become a partner with his father in the mercantile store, later also opening the Williams Hardware Store. According to the National Register report, Harrison Williams signed a warranty deed in 1883, giving the farm to the children; however, the family kept the farmstead intact until his death in 1906. Samuel Williams and his wife Frederica Welling Williams (daughter of Charles and Elizabeth Frizel Welling) and their family moved onto the farmstead in 1883. In 1909, he and his brother Joseph bought their siblings' portion of the estate, with Samuel keeping the property containing the farmhouse and outbuildings. Ownership was passed to Samuel's son George, then to Mary Kate Williams Johnson and brother G. Frederick Williams.

The Bollinger Family Cemetery

On a warm afternoon in July, when the temperature was 90-plus degrees, I was on my way home to Cape Girardeau after dropping off my granddaughters at their home in Fredericktown (of course, it just happens to be named for George), when I decided to make a detour. I wanted to visit Bollinger Mill and to hear what the park rangers had to say about Sarah and George. I was not disappointed. I heard many of the stories I already had uncovered, plus some more that I had not yet found. The park ranger told me about Ralph Daugherty's difficulties with the Bollinger family and his relationship to the founding of St. Vincent's Seminary and the beginnings of the Catholic Church in Cape, making me want to continue my history treasure hunt. I also wanted to visit the Bollinger Family Cemetery, which, in order to prevent vandalism, is not marked in any way. Directions were to cross the bridge, immediately turn right, and after just a short walk up the hill, I would find the cemetery. I was warned not to give up. I parked the car at the end of the road, took the bridge, turned right, and started up a slight hill.

Soon I found myself completely surrounded with woods on a path that had been made by rains washing small gulleys down the hill. I also realized that I was going into the woods and I was all alone. And the longer I walked, the steeper the hill grew. Just when I was about to give up and think maybe I was on the wrong trail, I met a couple coming down the hill. They assured me there was a cemetery in these woods and I was almost there. Finally, I arrived in a small

Bollinger Cemetery, Bollinger Mill State Park. *Photo by author.*

clearing, and there were the tombstones, some of which were almost two hundred years old. Many of the gravestones are very difficult to decipher.

A monument was erected by family in 1928, which contains, on the front side, the names and dates of the birth and death of family members buried there, the first being *Col. Geo. Frederick Bollinger, Born 1772, Died 1842.* Also buried in the cemetery are George's daughter Sarah, who died in 1882 at age eighty-three, and her two husbands, Joseph Frizel, who died in 1825, as well as Ralph Daugherty, who died in 1850. Ralph and Sarah's son Samuel Daugherty, age thirty-seven, who died March 2, 1865, is buried along with his wife Elizabeth, age thirty, who died January 1, 1863, and their daughter Bernice, age six, who died August 20, 1863. Joseph's mother Mary Langdon Frizel died in 1826 and is buried there with Sarah Josephine Frizel, age fifty-six, who died on August 21, 1879. She was the daughter of Joseph and Sarah Frizel. Charles F. Williams, son of Berenice Daugherty and H.H.M. Williams lived only one year, dying October 24, 1848. Sarah Wellington was only three years and three months old when she died.

The reverse side of the monument has this inscription:

George Frederick Bollinger
Colonizer, statesman, soldier, and patriot was born in Lincoln County, N.C. Married Elizabeth Hunsucker in 1798. Brought 20 families from N.C. to Cape Girardeau County in 1800, settling on White Water now Burfordville. Commissioned Major 4th Regiment Missouri Militia in 1812. Commissioned Lieutenant Colonel by Governor Clark in 1817.

~4~

A State Divided:

The Civil War Comes to Cape Girardeau County

When the Civil War began in 1861, Cape Girardeau was a quiet town of six thousand people, its boundaries being Washington Street north, Henderson Street west, and Jefferson Street south, as well as the river to the east. As in many border state towns, Cape Girardeau was split between the two sides—North and South. Southeast Missouri was made up of three-fourths Americans mostly from the Southern states and one-fourth recent German immigrants. Its division was reflected in the volunteer troops raised in the area. A Northern supporter, Lieutenant Colonel Lindsay Murdoch, raised four companies that were called the Fremont Rangers. A Jackson resident and Southern supporter, William L. Jeffers, a veteran of the Mexican War, organized cavalry troops called the Swamp Rangers in March 1861.

Joining this company of mounted volunteers was Dr. Samuel S. Harris, who would become the husband of Julia Russell in 1880. Dr. Harris was elected First Lieutenant. He commanded the McDowell battery at the Battle of Fredericktown on October 21, 1861. After leaving the Missouri State Guard, he organized Harris's Missouri Light Artillery, who manned the guns on the CSS Arkansas and played a key role in the war on the river in sinking the Union ironclad USS Carondelet, helping to break the siege of Vicksburg. He continued to resign from one command and organize another, serving at one time as an assistant surgeon for Jeffers' Eighth Missouri Cavalry Regiment until late 1863. He stayed with the wounded and was taken prisoner at Hartville and Cape Girardeau during Gen. John S. Marmaduke's raids into Missouri in 1863. He rode with Marmaduke again during the Price Expedition in 1864, surrendering his command at the rank of captain in Louisiana in June 1865, then returning to Cape Girardeau after a short stay in Mississippi.

According to the *National Register of Historic Places Nomination Form* for the former home of George Christian Thilenius, Thilenius was one of the Cape Girardeau County residents who supported the Union cause during the Civil War, as well as being a staunch abolitionist. At the time his views were unpopular since Southeast Missouri was predominantly pro-slavery. A native of Germany, Thilenius and his family fled to America after being involved in a failed revolution seeking to unite Germany under a liberal democratic government. The family settled in St. Louis where they opened a mercantile store. In 1853, George went to Cuba, where he spent three years working in sugar refining, then moved to Cape Girardeau where he was a partner in a mercantile store. Thilenius, along with a large group of German immigrants, joined Captain Lyon's forces to secure the city of St. Louis. He helped organize four local German companies in the Missouri Militia, being elected the First Lieutenant of Company A. He rose to the rank of colonel during the war. He was a delegate to the Drake Convention in January 1865, signing an ordinance passed by the delegates abolishing slavery in Missouri.

After the war, he became famous for the quality of the flour from his mill, Cape Girardeau Roller Mill, winning the Medal of Merit in Vienna's World's Fair in 1873 as well as the first prize at the Centennial Exposition in Philadelphia in 1876. He was instrumental in bringing the Normal School, now Southeast Missouri State University, to Cape Girardeau, served three terms as mayor of Cape Girardeau from 1867 to 1873, founded a German-American bank, and was involved in getting a railroad line through the town. Upon completion of his beautiful home, Longview, he constructed a winery on the property which, in addition to wine, produced the first "soda pop" in Cape. Thilenius served in the Missouri General Assembly, where he was a supporter of public education.

The first shots of the war were fired at Fort Sumter on April 11, 1861, and 3,000 of the Union's forces began occupying Cape Girardeau in August 1861, remaining until the end of the war. *Frank Leslie's Illustrated Newspaper* from New York, dated September 28, 1861, described Cape Girardeau as "about 45 miles north-west of Cairo, and 160 miles south-east of St. Louis, 1,180 from New Orleans, 860 from St. Paul, Minn. It is also the terminus of the road which leads to Jackson, the capital of the county, and to Fredericktown, and from thence to Pilot Knob and Ironton. It thus forms the landing point where troops and supplies can be sent from Cairo to Central Missouri." The writer points out that when the county seat was moved from Cape Girardeau to Jackson, the town dwindled but was improving due to the stream sawmill, as well as the excellent landing area on the river. The article is accompanied by a full-page, wood-engraved view entitled: "CAPE GIRARDEAU, MISS[ouri], AN IMPORTANT STRATEGIC POSITION ON THE MISSISSIPPI, BETWEEN CAIRO AND ST. LOUIS, NOW OCCUPIED BY THE U.S. FORCES." The picture shows the Union soldiers encamped at Fort A on the bluff on Bellevue Street, overlooking the village of Cape Girardeau, and shows homes, stores, a hotel, the courthouse, a windmill, Saint Vincent's Young Ladies Academy, Saint Vincent's Seminary, and boats on the river. The tents of the troops dot the bluff. Some soldiers are at attention, some at rest, but most are engaged with shovels and wheelbarrows in the process of building the fort. Such newspaper pictures were very popular during the Civil War, showing details of the soldiers and their war engagements.

When Major General John C. Fremont came to Cape Girardeau for an inspection, he commanded that four forts be built immediately for protection. The Southeast Missouri State University Archives has in its collection the letter sent by Major General Fremont to Captain Henry Flad, dated August 19, 1861, appointing him captain of the Engineer Corps, his new rank and pay dating from August 1, 1861. Flad was directed to proceed to Cape Girardeau to oversee the erection of fortifications and to complete the project as soon as possible. Fremont also promised two hundred laborers to work with the force already there. Later, when General Grant arrived in Cape Girardeau, having been urged by Fremont to promote the work of the forts, Grant reported that the fortifications at Cape Girardeau were "being pushed forward with vigor." George Thilenius was the organizer of a team of 110 local civilians, made up mostly of Germans, to construct the 4 Cape Girardeau forts. The forts were built in the French bastion design, a triangle with open base. Fort A was on a bluff at what is now Bellevue Street between Lorimier Street and Spanish Street, overlooking the river. Fort B was on the hill where Kent Library of Southeast Missouri State University now stands. It was armed with howitzers and 24-pound siege guns. Fort C was at the intersection of South Ellis Street and Good Hope Street, guarding the approach up Bloomfield Road, Gordonville Road, and Commerce Road on the south (now Sprigg Street). Finally, there was Fort D located farther south on the river bluff, which was the most important defense position in the area. Cape Girardeau was the first high ground on the Mississippi River in Missouri. The first military operation to fortify and hold it would have control of a significant part of the

Wood-engraved view of Fort A from Bellevue Street in Cape Girardeau during the Civil War. *From* Frank Leslie's Illustrated Newspaper, *September 28, 1861.*

river, as well as an opening into the heart of Missouri. Cannons were mounted there as well as at Fort A to control traffic on the Mississippi. The fort, located at Fort Street and Locust Street, has been restored with the original earthwork walls and a stone building on the original site of the powder house.

In hopes of speeding up the building of the forts, engineers Henry Flad and Franz Kappner were both assigned to the Cape Girardeau fort. Flad, a captain of engineers in Germany, fled his homeland for America, arriving in New York City in 1849, to avoid a sentence of death that had been pronounced against him for his part in revolutionary activities. After working as an engineer in the Northeast for several years, he went west to Missouri and worked on the Iron Mountain Railroad until the beginning of the Civil War, when he enlisted in the Union Army in June 1861. Within two years he had advanced all the way to colonel in the Engineer Regiment of the West. He was indispensable in moving General Grant's army of one hundred thousand troops over roads, bridges, and railroads. After the war he served as the chief assistant engineer for Captain James B. Eads for the seven-year construction of the Eads Bridge, as well as the designing of Forest Park in St. Louis. He became the first president of the board of public improvements in St. Louis from

1877–1890, when U.S. President Benjamin Harrison appointed him to the Mississippi River Commission.

The most prominent individual involved in the affairs of Cape Girardeau during the war was General Ulysses S. Grant, who would later become president of the United States. The story of General Grant's stay in Cape Girardeau is recounted in the *Riverboat Times*— the menu of the Port Cape Restaurant down by the Mississippi River. Cape Girardeau tradition holds that the building where the restaurant is located on the southwest corner of Water Street and Themis Street served as Grant's headquarters in Cape Girardeau, and that he stayed in the St. Charles Hotel, which was on the next block at the southwest corner of Main Street and Themis Street, until the headquarters were moved to Cairo, Illinois.

The following account is taken from the book, *Ulysses S. Grant— Memoirs and Selected Letters*. Grant had been in command in Jefferson City, Missouri, and was suddenly relieved of his duties on August 28, 1861, in a communication from Major General John C. Fremont. This letter can be found in the *War of the Rebellion,* seventy volumes of the most extensive collection of primary sources giving the history of the war from both sides of the conflict. With the collection of ma-

Colonel Henry Flad, engineer of the forts constructed in Cape Girardeau during the Civil War. *From* Guide to the Henry Flad Papers circa 1855–1978, *courtesy of Southeast Missouri State University Archives.*

terials begun in 1864, the historical set consists of firsthand accounts, orders, reports, maps, diagrams, and letters.

Fremont instructed Grant to proceed to Cape Girardeau and assume command of the district of Southeast Missouri covering all of the area in Missouri south of St. Louis, as well as southern Illinois. Grant arrived in Cape Girardeau at 4:30 P.M. on August 30, 1861. In his memoirs Grant says:

> In pursuance of my orders I established my temporary head-quarters at Cape Girardeau and sent instructions to the commanding officer at Jackson, to inform me of the approach of General Prentiss from Ironton. . . . Neither General Prentiss nor Colonel Marsh, who commanded at Jackson, knew their destination. I drew up all of the instructions for the contemplated move, and kept them in my pocket until I should hear of the junction of our troops at Jackson. Two or three days after my arrival at Cape Girardeau, word came that General Prentiss was approaching that place [Jackson]. I started at once to meet him there and give him his orders. As I turned the first corner of the street after starting, I saw a column of calvary [sic] passing the next street in front of me. I turned and rode around the block the other way, so as to meet the head of the column. I found there General Prentiss himself, with a large escort. He had halted his troops at Jackson for the night, and had come on himself to Cape Girardeau, leaving orders for his command to follow him on the morning.

On the same day that Grant received the communication from Fremont as to his new assignment, Brigadier General Prentiss, who had expected the appointment himself, had also received a letter from Fremont informing him that Grant, as he appeared on the official list, outranked Prentiss and would take command of the whole expedition. General Prentiss raised the issue of rank with Grant, finally refusing to obey orders from Grant and putting himself under arrest. In a letter to Prentiss, Grant declined to place Prentiss under arrest, while Prentiss proceeded to St. Louis under General Fremont's orders. Grant stated he had acted from duty and had no personal feeling against Prentiss. He was "perfectly willing to see the charges quashed and the whole matter buried in oblivion." On September 4, 1861, Grant moved his headquarters to Cairo. This confrontation between Grant and Prentiss is commemorated on the Mississippi River Tales Mural on the river wall in downtown Cape.

The Battle of Cape Girardeau

Cape Girardeau was the scene of its lone Civil War battle on April 26, 1863, when Confederate General John S. Marmaduke and his 5,000 cavalrymen were sent to Missouri to make a raid in order to get provisions and to capture Cape Girardeau. His was a motley crew that was ill-trained and ill-equipped. According to Marmaduke's report on the expedition in a communiqué written May 20, 1863, which can be found in the *War of the Rebellion*, their weapons included eight pieces of field artillery, two light mountain pieces, shotguns, Enfield or Mississippi rifles, and even squirrel rifles. Of the 5,000 men, 1,200 were unarmed and 900 had no horses. Marmaduke's reasoning in taking the unarmed and dismounted was the hope of capturing weapons and horses, along with the fear that if he did not take them, they would desert. The Confederates advanced on Cape Girardeau from a line from present-day St. Mary's cemetery, the area of Capaha Park, and Central Junior High School, to Bloomfield Road. The main attack was near the intersection of present-day Perryville Road and Broadway. The Confederates were caught in a cross fire between the guns of Fort B (Kent Library) and batteries of

Confederate General John S. Marmaduke (left). *Photo courtesy of Library of Congress.* Brigadier General John McNeil (right), Union commander at the Battle of Cape Girardeau. *Public domain photo.*

artilleries planted on the hill where Southeast Hospital is now. As the battle in the valley went on, steamboat whistles announced the arrival of reinforcements by river. Finally, General Marmaduke called for a retreat. The battle lasted only four to five hours and turned out to be more of a skirmish than a battle. Expecting an attack, General John McNeil had ordered the women and children of the town evacuated by steamboat to a safe place upstream on the night of April 25. Reports on dead and wounded vary, with one count being Union, 23 dead and 14 wounded. Marmaduke, in his report at the end of the expedition into Missouri, estimated 30 dead, 60 wounded, and 120 missing. He also reported a gain of 150 recruits and improvement in horses for the troops. He erroneously estimated that the Federal loss must have exceeded the Confederate losses by at least five times.

A very detailed description of the Battle of Cape Girardeau appeared in *The New York Daily Tribune*, Friday, May 1, 1863, written by a correspondent named Guilbert. Headlines proclaimed:

BATTLE OF CAPE GIRARDEAU
Army of Marmaduke with 10,000 Men! The Place Defended by Brig.-Gen. John McNiel with 2,000 Men for Five Hours!- The Enemy Repulsed with Great Slaughter!
[Note: The number of Confederates seems to be greatly exaggerated in comparison with estimates from other sources.]

Guilbert writes:

> During the battle I had taken my position with the artillerists in fort B, where, from the great eminence of the fort, I beheld the whole scene in its awful sublimity—saw the flash of the cannon, witnessed the fall of killed and wounded men, and heard the roar of the dread artillery shake the heavens and the solid ground. At first as I went out toward the fort [B] a mingled sense of awe and fear came over me, but the fascination of the scene drew me on, till, when I had got among the men, and saw their cheerful and determined courage, and heard their deafening cheers and cries, all sense of fear was lost, and the impulse became almost irresistible to take up a weapon and step into the ranks.

Guilbert also mentioned that patriotic citizens of Cape, all of them German, brought their shotguns and rifles and participated in the battle. On the other hand, he noted that several native-born

Cape Girardeau males joined the women and children on the boat for safety on the other side of the river.

Guilbert praised Captain N.S. Green, the captain of the steamboat *Mary Forsyth*, who

> took every pains to receive and accommodate all the women and children who came on board. They filled his cabin to overflowing, and he gave them mattresses and places to sleep, and food, and kept them on his boat two nights and nearly two days, showing them the utmost consideration and kindness, being himself also detained from an important trip to Memphis, and obliged to land much of his freight on the Illinois shore.

Guilbert's report listed the totals for the battle as Confederates, sixty killed and three hundred wounded; Union, six killed and one wounded. At the end of the article, Guilbert closes with a note that he is steaming his way down the river on the *Mary Forsyth* to Cairo where he will post his report.

The property on which Fort B sat, owned by Michael Dittlinger, before the war contained the *Dittlinger and Bro.* lime kilns and quarry. An artist's drawing of the site done about 1861 can be seen on the large mural at the Cape River Heritage Museum. In the picture, the Dittlingers' brick home is perched on the hill where Kent Library is presently located, with the steep walls at the foot of the hill surrounding the quarry where the Southeast football stadium is now. A cooper's shop for making barrel staves can be seen along with the lime kilns that are belching smoke. The hillsides surrounding the home were covered in orchards, vineyards, gardens, and dense woods.

In the 1976 bicentennial publication *Biography of Historic Cape Girardeau County*, Ann Dittlinger writes about the use of the house in the war years. She quotes Colonel G.C. Thilenius about the property:

> Michael Dittlinger lived right up on top of the hill. The property was used for a fortification during the war. The house was made a part of the fortification, which was put up right alongside the house on both sides, taking in the house. Fort B they called that. He had no possession of the house; it was taken by the military and used as long as they used the fortification.

Michael Dittlinger was a senior first lieutenant of Company F, Second Illinois Artillery, Powell's battery, and fought at Corinth,

The property of Michael Dittlinger, which was confiscated during the Civil War for the location of Fort B. *Photo courtesy of Cape River Heritage Museum.*

Pittsburg Landing, and Shiloh under Grant. In a letter dated March 1862, he wrote: "My dwelling house is situated in Fort B, as you know and my family without protection when I am gone."

A company of soldiers took over the cooper's shop for a kitchen and burned the barrel staves for fuel. The trees were cut down for firewood, while the orchard trees were pulled up by their roots and along with dirt thrown up on the west and south sides of the house, making it part of the fort.

Colonel Thilenius described the battle from Fort B:

> Marmaduke attacked this place and we used our 24-pounders. We dismantled their guns. None of the shots passed through the house, but the cannonading damaged the house considerable. The walls were cracked and the whole place ruined, you might say, the terraces and everything else.

After the war the house and grounds were restored to their original state at much expense and time.

Dr. Samuel S. Harris served with Jeffers' Regiment, Missouri Cavalry, as the Assistant Surgeon during the Battle of Cape Girardeau. The following communication sent by him to Jeffers is found in the *War of the Rebellion.*

Report of Asst. Surg. S. S. Harris, Jeffers' Missouri Regiment (Confederate).

JEFFERS' REGIMENT,
Camp near Wittsburg, Ark., May 27, 1863

SIR: By your order, I was left with Drs. (John F.) Yancey and (J. F.) Brookheart in charge of our wounded after the withdrawal of our forces from Cape Girardeau.

Inclosed [*sic*] is a report of our wounded.

I asked for permission of the Federal authorities to establish our hospital in or near Cape Girardeau. The request was not granted, and our wounded were removed to their post hospital....

Report of wounded in the fight before Cape Girardeau
Major 1, Lieutenant 1, Captain 1, Privates 18

I was not permitted to visit the battle-field [in Cape]; but, from the best information I could obtain, there were only 3 killed on the field. I could not learn their names or command. They were buried by our friends.

Of the five nurses that remained, two only were permitted to stay with our wounded, and the others were sent to Saint Louis as prisoners of war.

When I left Cape Girardeau our wounded were well cared for, and had everything requisite to make them comfortable.

Respectfully, yours, &c.

S. S. HARRIS,

Assistant surgeon, Provisional Army of the Confederate States

The surgeons were then furnished with an escort to Bloomfield, where they were to be returned to their unit. However, when General McNeil arrived, he took the men back to Cape Girardeau, keeping them for five days, and then sent them on their way to Little Rock where they would find General Price's command. McNeil's reasoning was that the demand for the surrender of Cape Girardeau was made by Colonel Carter under the command of General Price; therefore, he would send them to Price.

Harris asked for and was given a copy of the surrender order, which he forwarded to Jeffers. It was dated April 25, 1863, from

G.W. Carter, Commander, Fourth Division, First Army Corps, Trans-Mississippi Department, and stated, "Sir: By order of Maj. Gen. Sterling Price, commanding, I formally demand of you the immediate surrender, unconditionally, of the troops in Cape Girardeau and the adjoining forts, together with all the ammunition, stores, and other property belonging to the United States in the same." In the case of surrender, Colonel Carter pledged to treat the troops as prisoners of war and to protect private property. General McNeil received the demand by a flag of truce at 2:00 A.M. on April 26, with a time limit for surrender within half an hour, which was declined.

The Sherwood-Minton Home at 444 Washington Street was used as a hospital during the war, mainly for the smallpox outbreak. It was built for Reverend and Mrs. Adreil Sherwood in 1846 to be used as a private home and day school. Sherwood taught literature and languages to young men. At the outbreak of the war, the home was owned by Matthew H. Moore, a lawyer and the publisher of the *Cape Girardeau Eagle,* a weekly newspaper that advocated secession. The paper was turned to pro-Union at the beginning of the war. An unfortunate incident occurred causing Moore's departure.

Two drunken Union soldiers with the Twentieth Illinois Regiment, who were occupying Cape Girardeau, insulted Moore's attractive young daughter. Outraged citizens reported the incident to Colonel Marsh, the regimental commander, who ordered the men to march for two hours in the streets of Cape Girardeau wearing signs front and back that said: "These are curs who insult women," after which they were thrown in prison.

Rumors continue to circulate about the house being haunted, as well as having secret tunnels leading to the river from the basement of the house that were used for escaping slaves and by Union soldiers.

The Sherwood-Minton house served as a hospital during the Civil War. *Photo by author.*

An interesting supplement to the *War of Rebellion* series is volume 77, which records the events of the Eighteenth U.S. Colored Infantry. Company A was first mustered into service in Kansas City, where they worked on the telegraph, then sent by steamboat to Cape Girardeau, where they arrived in May 1864 for the purpose of organizing and recruiting. Company B arrived at Cape Girardeau on April 30 without officers or arms. There they drilled, did garrison duty, and recruited. In June 1864, the companies moved on by steamboat to New Madrid, Missouri.

Southeast Missouri Remembers the Civil War

Federal Writers' Project 1935–1942

In the years from 1935–1942, the United States Works Project Administration sponsored a Federal Writers' Project engaging 300 writers in 24 states to produce 2,900 documents. Writers assigned to the Folklore Project compiled and transcribed life histories.

In 1937, Mollie E. Smith, a reporter for the Federal Writers' Project, interviewed Mr. Frederick Monroe Davis who, as far as was known, was the last surviving Cape Girardeau County Civil War veteran who defended the forts at Cape Girardeau. He was born in West Virginia in 1845, later moving with his parents to Cape Girardeau County in the Gravel Hill area near Oak Ridge. He was ninety-three years of age when interviewed.

In early 1863, at age eighteen, Davis enlisted in the Union army under Colonel Thilenius, serving as a corporal in Company A, commanded by Captain Shawnee Bill Wilson, while stationed at Fort D for the rest of the war. In the interview, he described life at the fort. "We had two big cannons in the fort, one at each corner overlooking the river, but the soldiers got a lot of logs and painted them and made them look like cannons as they stuck over the earthwork. [These were called 'Quaker cannons', named after the pacifist religious sect.] The gunboats saw us and wouldn't come any further up the river than the fort." Within the fort, the soldiers lived in tents, providing their entertainment by playing cards or having wrestling matches. Davis remembered one wrestling match in which he and another soldier, who was quite small, were chosen by the officers to wrestle with a large bully named Tom Berry, who had bragged about being able to defeat any two men in the company. The match between the three men was to begin at the drop of a hat; however, when the hat fell, the small man didn't join in, but even without his partner, Davis was able to down the bully in the end.

Another form of entertainment was holding a company dance in the town. On one occasion, Davis's company took over another company's dance until the soldiers holding the dance began taking one after another of Davis's company out and beating them up. Davis was in a side room with a girl. He said to her, "Now what am I going to do? She said 'Do? Why, your time is next.' I was sitting near a window and I dived right through it. . . . and made my escape. That was one licking I got out of."

His company did not see much fighting, but mostly went out for skirmishes, scouting, or foraging for food. After the battle of Pilot Knob, Davis's company was "detailed to clear off the battlefield, take care of the wounded and remove the dead." Davis tells about burying the dead in trenches. He reported seeing about forty dead horses on the scene. When he ran into Confederate soldiers Will Byrd and Will Forkins, whom he knew, who were with an officer whose legs had been shot away, he walked up to them and said, "Consider yourselves under arrest and hand over your guns . . . After awhile Byrd and Forkins said they were going to a nearby farmhouse for dinner— so I said I'd go too. As we were sitting at the table, the woman of the house said that was one thing she never expected to see—soldiers from both sides sitting down eating peaceably at the same table." After the meal, the two Confederates were made to take an oath to leave the fighting and were sent home. In the days following the war's end, any time Davis met Mr. Will Byrd on the streets of Jackson, Byrd always made a sharp remark about that day.

From the Federal Writers' Project, Nov. 2, 1937, author unknown:

> The town of Jackson suffered greatly during the war, but not as greatly as many towns in the locality. Interesting stories are told of these days. A short distance southwest of Jackson a band of Confederate guerrillas overtook a Union supply company, carrying supplies from Cape Girardeau to Bloomfield. All the federal soldiers were killed, wagons burned, and mules slaughtered. Just south of there on Whitewater River, a company of Confederates were preparing to cook supper when they were surprised by a detachment of Union soldiers who fired on the camp. The first shots struck a sack of flour and the soldiers escaped in a cloud formed by the flying flour. One man jumped in the river. He could not swim and crawled on the bottom and escaped on the other side. This man lived in Jackson many years after the war and told the story frequently.

Mrs. Glenn Hope, who lived at 616 Bellevue in Cape Girardeau, related two stories about the Civil War days, which she had heard from her father-in-law Mr. C.H. Hope, who was a Confederate soldier.

On one occasion Mr. Hope slipped home to see his wife and family who lived on a farm. The Federals heard that he was there and came in search of him, but he slipped out in time, hid in [the] corn field and escaped. Mrs. Hope had money in a bag hidden underneath her long full dress skirt. She knew the soldiers suspected that she had money so she just sat and rocked and knitted while they searched for her husband. They even looked in the churn, and she calmly remarked, knowing all the time that they were searching for money as well as for Mr. Hope, "Well, he is a little large to hide in there."

Mrs. Hope's second story was related to Confederate Colonel William Jeffers. His wife Josephine, the daughter of Sarah Abernathy, would often accompany her husband during the early days of the war, and on the occasion of a battle, her brother would be detailed to care for her. After she returned home, Jeffers came for a visit, but upon hearing that Union soldiers were approaching, made his escape. When the soldiers came in to search for Jeffers, Mrs. Abernathy stood firmly in front of the stairs, refusing the soldiers entry "over my dead body" since her daughters were in bed and no men were allowed. She then called to her daughters to get up and dress, only then allowing the soldiers to search. Of course, they found nothing.

During the Civil War, the Common Pleas courthouse served as the headquarters for the Union provost marshal who was the military governor. The dungeon under the courthouse was used for locals not loyal to the Union, captured rebels, Union soldiers breaking army rules, and others waiting to stand trial. John Fugate Bolin was a Rebel guerrilla who had been imprisoned for allegedly murdering unarmed Union supporters. In a *Southeast Missourian* article entitled "Looking Backward," dated July 10, 1926, and included in the Federal Writers' Project, is an interview with Mr. W.A. Bacon, a native of old Appleton and a veteran of the Civil War. While he was resting in Courthouse Park during the interview, he recalled the mob of soldiers and local people who took Bolin from the courthouse dungeon and hanged him on the gatepost on Bloomfield Road where it crosses Henderson.

Another interviewee for the Federal Writers' Project told about the disturbing experience of observing an execution during the war. "I saw a man shot at Fort C. There were six guns—they weren't all loaded, nobody knew which were blanks. The man to be killed sat on a coffin with a piece of paper over his heart as a target for the leveled guns. I was only six or seven years old and could not sleep for a long time because of the horror at this deed."

Ex-Slave Narratives

During the years 1936–1938 more than 2,300 accounts of ex-slave narratives, along with 500 black-and-white pictures, were recorded by the Federal Writers' Project. One of those interviewed was Smoky Eulenberg, who was born October 13, 1854. When a slave, he lived about three miles from Jackson on the farm owned by his master Henry Walker in a large house of logs with a wide open hall in between the rooms on either side. Smoky said that his father was Solomon Eulenberg, "a big fine looking man," and that his mother had come from Tennessee when she was ten years old. Walker had nearly a hundred slaves and about twelve cabins in the quarters.

Smoky said that none of Walker's slaves ever tried to run away. "We had a good home and we all stayed till dey declare peace and lots of us kept on a staying cause we didn't know nothing else to do. But my father was industrious. He worked hard and saved his money and in a couple of years he bought a team and we moved to a little place."

Smoky made several references to the soldiers in the area. Many times they saw the soldiers passing by, but the soldiers never mistreated anyone except to come in and eat food that had been prepared or ask the cook to make more.

He remembered on a Sunday morning that a group of Union soldiers came by telling about burning the mill at Burfordville. That would have been the Bollinger Mill. Another day a bunch of Rebels came by and camped about a mile from their home. During the night the "bluecoats" killed about thirty of the Rebels.

He recalled some good times when growing up. "Us boys played marbles and ball and other games like boys will. On Saturday from 5–9 we all had off. Den we'd congregate and have singing and dancing. At Christmas and such days we'd have a big time."

He remembered an amusing story about one time when his mother refused to be sold.

> I rec'lect one time missus sold my mother and four children but it wasn't no trade. De woman's name was Mrs. Shepard and

she was a sassy old woman. She come into my mother's cabin and grabbed her and told her she was going to take her home. Mother jes pushed her out the door and said she wouldn't go—and she told missus she wouldn't go—so dey had to call it off—it was no trade.

James Goings, another ex-slave who, at the time of his interview, lived at the end of Bodean Lane in Cape, was the son of Teresa Cannon, who belonged to old Dr. Cannon of Jackson, and Tom Goings, who lived on a nearby plantation. Teresa and James were bought by Mrs. Dunn and later Lige Hill, whose farm was near Whitewater. James was about ten years old when the war was over. Teresa lived to be 115 years of age.

Family Stories

During the Civil War, Linus Sanford of Jackson was age twenty-three when the war began. He was the son of Henry Sanford and later the husband of Martha Jane "Mattie" Russell. The following story is related in *Clyde Arthur and Julia Sanford Vandivort of Cape Girardeau, Missouri, Their Ancestors and Descendents*:

> A Wisconsin Regiment was stationed in Cape Girardeau during the Civil War…The Regiment had as one of its spies a local man whose name was B. Taylor. When this man was found to be missing, the regiment picked up eight or ten men on the town square at Jackson, Missouri, and brought them over to Cape Girardeau, putting them in prison. The Union Commander announced that these men would be held in prison until B. Taylor's killers were produced.
>
> After holding the group for a few days and feeling that they were not getting the information they wanted, the officers of the Wisconsin Regiment had the Jackson men draw lots to see who were to be shot in case B. Taylor was not found. Linus Sanford and Joseph Schmuke were the two men who were to be shot.
>
> Sanford and Schmuke were imprisoned in the old dungeons that were under the Common Pleas Court House in Cape Girardeau. They spent many months in prison and suffered many hardships, but they were not executed nor was B. Taylor found. Later the Wisconsin Troops moved on without having decided what to do about these two men. When Nebraska Troops came to replace the Wisconsin troops in Cape Girardeau and took

charge, they tried these two men, Linus Sanford and Joseph Schmuke, and both were released. The two men were so weakened that they were unfit for service during the remainder of the war and suffered poor health the rest of their lives. Vandivort family oral history is that the Nebraska regiment that was responsible for the release of Linus Sanford had one or several officers who had attended Harvard with him and that they were the persons responsible for his release.

In the March 20, 1974, issue of the *Jackson Post and Cash-Book*, Mrs. Elizabeth Wilson, a great-great-granddaughter of George Frederick Bollinger and a "veritable encyclopedia of family lore," relates several anecdotes about her great-great-grandmother Sarah. The stories were told to her by her grandmother, Elizabeth Frizel Welling, a daughter of Sarah Bollinger Frizel Daugherty.

> Sarah's sons Samuel and Frederick were avid Confederate supporters and their mother's sympathies were entirely with them. However, they had to exercise discreteness, as this area's residents were deeply divided on the war's issues . . . Late one night during the war, Mrs. Wilson's Grandmother Welling was surprised to hear voices coming from the living room. On investigation, she found her mother, Sarah, and stepbrothers, Fred and Sam Daugherty, sitting in complete darkness discussing plans to deliver flour and meal to the Confederate forces. They could not risk being seen together in the daylight.
>
> In another incident during the War, the northern soldiers discovered that Fred and Sam Daugherty were supplying southern troops with flour and meal from their mother's mill. A regiment was sent out to Burfordville to seek retaliation. A cannon was set up on the east bank of the river and was utilized in a vain attempt to destroy the dam George Frederick Bollinger had built in 1825. Infuriated by their failure, the soldiers managed to burn most of the mill. Much of the heavy wood timbers survived the holocaust though.
>
> The blue-uniformed troops then moved in on the Old Bollinger homestead, where Sarah, then about 65 years old, was residing. Carrying lighted torches, they ordered her out of the house. She refused. The commander, caught by complete surprise, resorted to name calling, terming her a witch. Sarah, shouting from an upstairs window, said, "So burn the house, that's what they do to witches, so burn it." This must have

completely befuddled the soldiers, as they left the house and Mrs. Daugherty quite intact. Mrs. Wilson pointed out this exchange originated from an elderly woman who was only about 4'10" tall. Sarah went on to live to be 81 years old, which was quite an age for those years. Like Mrs. Wilson said, "She was quite a gal."

In 1974, Mrs. Wilson and her sister, Mrs. Mildred Hartsfield, lived in the house at 209 West Main Street, in Jackson, the house that has been in the family except for a few years since *circa* 1818 when Joseph Frizel built it for his bride, Sarah Bollinger. In 1838, Charles Welling bought the property, which Joseph Frizel had sold in 1821, and built an addition to it for his new bride, Elizabeth Frizel, the daughter of Sarah and Joseph Frizel. Elizabeth had been born in the house on January 31, 1820. The new wing was in the Greek Revival style. So the house was once again back in family ownership. The home was the scene of many interesting family stories. A short-lived Masonic lodge was organized there by Joseph and Alexander Buckner, with Sarah helping with the painting of symbols on the aprons. The planning meeting between Sarah and her sons about food for the Confederates occurred here. The first public library in Jackson was organized and opened in the Frizel wing of the house in 1926. The organizational meetings for both the First Presbyterian Church of Jackson and the Jackson Academy were held in the house. According to family tradition, slaves slept in the loft over the kitchen, but the loft was eliminated after the Civil War. The house was placed on the National Register of Historic Places in 1999.

Sarah's sons were wounded in the war, and after her sons died and Sarah could no longer operate the mill by herself, she sold the property to S.H. Burford and moved back to Jackson. In 1865, the mill was rebuilt, using bricks molded from clay near the river. The top floor was used for the village school. The name of the village was changed to Burfordville. Sarah Bollinger Daugherty died at the residence of her daughter Mary Russell in Jackson, Missouri, on Friday, April 21, 1882. She was eighty-two years of age.

Julia Russell Harris would have been thirteen, her sister Mattie fifteen, and brother James eleven when the war began and would have heard and even experienced many family stories to pass along to future generations. Their mother Mary Frizel Russell and their grandmother, Sarah Bollinger Daugherty, being widows, probably had many challenges in the trying days during the war as well as afterwards. Their situation reminded me of my own family stories of the war.

The Welling home, standing at 209 West Main Street in Jackson, was built in 1818 for Sarah Bollinger by her husband Joseph Frizel. In 1838, Welling bought the home, building an addition for his new bride, the Frizels' daughter, born there in 1820. *Photo courtesy of Jackson Heritage Association.*

My great-grandmother, Annie Eliza Sumners Bolton, wrote an autobiography which included her memories of the Civil War. "Grandma Bolton," as she was fondly called by family, was born in Franklin County, Alabama, on March 11, 1851, and would have been age ten when the war began. She wrote her memories on May 12, 1930, at age seventy-nine. She recalled the election of Abraham Lincoln in 1860, when she would have been age five, and the excitement, as well as the talk of war that the election generated.

She describes the coming of war:

> Young as I was I had a perfect horror of war. . . . My father enlisted in the southern army in August, 1861. And was wounded in the famous battle of Shiloh. He came home and remained until he had parcially [*sic*] recovered from his wound. And then returned to the army, and was never at home any more. The battle of Shiloh was near enough to our home that we could hear the cannonading all day it was a sad [day] indeed. For we felt sure that our dear father, and many of our friends were engaged in the battle. If I mistake not that was April 1862. And our dear father was killed at the battle of Murfreesboro Tenn. about the first of January 1863.

Our dear mother was left with seven children ranging in age

from two years to seventeen. The eldest being a son and when he was just a little more than seventeen, he enlisted in the army and served till the close of the war. Our mother was never very strong. And had never had to work in the field. But during that cruel war she had to work in the field and often had to follow the plow to make bread for us children and herself. With all the hardships she had to undergo it was to [sic] much for her delicate constitution and soon she became an invalid, and only lived nine year [sic] after our father's death.

Other Stories

On November 23, 2010, an unusual story was published in the *Southeast Missourian* about Washington Giboney, a black man who traveled from Cape Girardeau to Michigan, where he joined the Union Army, serving with the 102nd Colored Infantry. After the war he returned to Cape Girardeau to live, which was probably difficult considering the number of Southern sympathizers who lived in Cape. He is buried at the Shady Grove Cemetery near Dutchtown.

In *Stories of Cape Girardeau*, Allan Hinchey related an event that happened many years after the war ended. The two elderly daughters of James Reynolds sat on the porch of the historic home on North Main Street on an August afternoon in 1912 and spoke of remembrances of the War Between the States. As they recalled their father's burying of a sack of silver in a very deep hole, they suddenly remembered where the silver had been buried. They grabbed their tools and began digging, uncovering a large earthen jar, which for fifty years had held a treasure valued at $1,200.

The website of the Southeast Regional Planning Commission notes that when the Civil War began, the Union of the Confederacy instituted conscription; however, slave owners with more than twenty slaves were not required to serve. Since St. Mary's of the Barrens Seminary in Perryville had a good reputation, the sons of Southern landowners were sent to the school not only for an education but also to protect them from the possible dangers of war. One of the teachers, Father Abram J. Ryan, left his duties at the seminary to serve as a chaplain for the Confederate Army.

Today in Courthouse Park in Cape Girardeau stand two symbols of the division that existed in Missouri during the war years. One is a statue of a Union soldier standing atop a fountain. The idea for the memorial originated in 1901 with the Women's Relief Corps, an auxiliary of the Grand Army of the Republic, which was formed in 1866 to aid widows and orphans of soldiers and to honor the valor of Union soldiers. When the Corps disbanded, a group of ten women, one of whom was Mrs. W.H. Harrison, who along with her husband, was the owner of the house at 313 Themis, determined to complete the task. To raise the needed money, they sponsored card parties, boat excursions, festivals, and carnation sales on President McKinley's birthday. The local newspaper, the *Daily Republican,* aided the group with a special fountain issue. Although it took ten years to raise the money, the memorial was dedicated on May 30, 1911. The program for the dedication

Union and Confederate Monuments in Courthouse Park. *Photo by author.*

included a performance by the Schucherts' band, songs by the Normal Chorus and public school children, and a speech by Governor Herbert S. Hadley.

Beside the fountain stands a monument to the Confederate soldiers from Southeast Missouri, made from Georgia silver gray marble presented in 1931 by the Cape Girardeau Daughters of the Confederacy. This monument was originally in the median on Morgan Oak at the approach to the old Mississippi River bridge. In later years, it was moved to the Courthouse Park. A recent newcomer to the city of Cape Girardeau was surprised to see both memorials, Union and Confederate, there together, side by side, in the city park.

The Women of Bollinger: The Next Generation

Mattie and Linus Sanford

Sanford

Linus Sanford

married

Martha Jane Russell

Born to Linus and Martha

Linus Sanford   Julia Adele Sanford

Mattie Sanford

Julia Russell's older sister, Martha Jane "Mattie" Russell, married Linus Sanford on January 31, 1872, in the parlor of the Marble City Hotel located on the levee of the Mississippi River at the end of Broadway in Cape Girardeau. Mattie was twenty-six and Linus was thirty-three. Their wedding was described by "Dot" in the *Jackson Cash-Book Journal* dated February 2, 1872:

> On the evening of the 31st inst, [January] I received a special invitation to attend at the Marble City Hotel, at 8 P. M. sharp. Filled with wonder and doubt, I did so, and found the vast building one blaze of light, and fairly alive with strange faces. After being ushered into the spacious parlor, I had scarcely

noticed the surroundings, when Senator Greene and Louis Houck, Esq., were announced. [The writer goes on to name quite a few others who were present. One guest of note was Dr. S.S. Harris, who eight years later would wed Julia Russell.]

At half past eight the folding doors were opened and in the center of the adjoining room stood a table covered with ladies' work baskets, toilet stands, card-cases, vases, silver pitchers, goblets, fruit stands, sugar and butter dishes, spoons, forks, etc. and hid away beneath were packages of jewelry, from finger rings to bracelets, breastpins, eardrops, chains and clasps of every name and dimension. These were bridal presents. I had scarcely time to feast my eyes on the costly array, when the bridal party were announced—Rev. Dr. Samuels of St. Louis entered in full flowing clerical robes; he was followed by Hon. L. Sanford, and on his arm leaned blushing and trembling, dear little Miss Mattie Russell; they were followed by Mr.—[sic; probably her Uncle Charles] Russell and Miss Julia Russell. The party took their stand at the upper end of the parlor, when the Doctor faced the couple and offered up a feeling prayer; then proceeded the ceremony and Linus and Mattie were declared one. After the benediction, the happy couple were surrounded by a throng of friends and well-wishers.

Following the ceremony, the company was led by the newlyweds into the dining hall for a sumptuous feast, including the groom's and bride's cake. The party concluded about midnight. On the next morning, Mr. and Mrs. Sanford took the train to St. Louis for a few days. From there they traveled on to Jefferson City where Linus resumed his duties as the state representative from Cape Girardeau County.

On May 5, 1936, Mattie's granddaughter, Dorothy Virginia Vandivort, daughter of Julia and Clyde Vandivort, wore her grandmother's silk and point lace wedding gown, which her grandmother had worn sixty-five years before, as well as her great-great-grandmother's lace cap, as she was wed to Thomas Harvey Beadles at Christ Episcopal Church in Cape Girardeau. The reception was held at the Vandivort home at 504 Bellevue Street.

The same gown was worn again by Virginia's sister Patricia Vandivort on February 13, 1941, when she married Lieutenant Charles A Reissaus at Christ Episcopal. The *Southeast Missourian* article described it this way:

Miss Patricia Vandivort . . . wore for her wedding . . . the bridal gown of her grandmother, the late Mrs. Linus Sanford, carried a point lace handkerchief made by her great-grandmother, the late Mrs. Mary Russell, and had, to secure her veil, a cap which belonged to her great-great-grandmother, Mrs. Sarah Bollinger Frissel . . . The dress was of off-white, heavy old silk and the cap of heavy, cream-colored lace. Her veil of tulle trailed over the train of the dress and she carried a white prayer book with an orchid on top and white ribbon streamers . . .

The wedding gown and cap were donated to the Cape River Heritage Museum by Virginia Vandivort Beadles, who passed away in 2003.

Mattie and Linus's great-granddaughter, Martha Vandivort, the daughter of Mabel May Sanford and Sydney Tanner, shared the history of their family in an interview in the March 29, 2000, *Cash-Book Journal.* Linus's father Henry Sanford, who was born in Connecticut in 1794, taught school in Cape Girardeau and Jackson for four years before moving to Arkansas, where he became a circuit clerk. However, he returned to Jackson where he was the circuit clerk for Cape Girardeau County. Upon his death in 1861, Henry had held the office of circuit clerk from 1826–1861, with the exception of one term. Henry married Mary Daugherty, daughter of William Daugherty, granddaughter of Andrew Ramsey, and sister of Ralph Daugherty. About 1850, Henry and Mary Sanford built a stately Southern-style home overlooking Hubble Creek on the property north of the Jackson Square, which now has become the Jackson City Park. Henry and Mary were the parents of Pearl, born in 1830, who moved to Australia; Eli, who was born in 1833 and died of cholera; Theresa, born in 1834; and Linus, born January 1, 1839. Linus's lineage was traced by the family back to Richard Sanford of Essex and Much Hadham, Hertfordshire, England, who died in 1590. Also, Linus's great-grandfather, Andrew Ramsey, came to Cape Girardeau County in 1794, the first American settler in the Spanish regime.

Linus Sanford attended St. Vincent's Academy in Cape Girardeau and then graduated with a law degree from Harvard. He represented Cape Girardeau County in the state legislature, beginning his first term in 1872, when he and Mattie were wed. His law office remained in the Jackson Courthouse until his death at age seventy-three. Martha Vandivort said, "Many old-timers around Jackson told me you could set your watch by his comings and goings from lunch every day. He walked or rode his horse."

In 1878, Mattie and Linus moved into the home originally built by Linus's parents, which was described in an article in the Federal Writers' Project as "the scene of almost continuous gaiety, where they lived

Dorothy Virginia Vandivort in her grandmother Mattie's wedding gown, Christ Episcopal Church, May 5, 1936. *Photo courtesy of Cape River Heritage Museum.*

together and hosted many grand parties until Linus's death in 1912." Three children were born to Mattie and Linus: Linus Jr., 1873; Julia Adele, 1877; and Martha Jane ("Mattie"), 1883.

In the *Cash-Book* article, Martha Vandivort also shared information about family heirlooms in her home. A unique wedding gift from Linus to Mattie is a set of nine-inch vases, each one of them the life-size wrist and hand models of Queen Victoria. They are made of white porcelain called Parian Ware. Other family treasures are several pieces of needlework and quilts done by Mattie, one of which received a first place at the Southeastern District Agricultural Society.

Mattie and the Episcopal Church

In numerous articles in *The Church News*, a publication of the St. Louis Episcopal Diocese, Mattie Sanford is highly praised for her work in the small Church of the Redeemer in Jackson. In the March 1914 issue, she is described as the "mother in Israel" without whom the church in Jackson would be unknown. The Rev. J.J. Clopton goes on to state that:

> Jackson is happy in having fortnightly Sunday night services again and the Holy Communion month by month. For many

years, whether or not a pastor were nominally in charge of Jackson, Mrs. Linus Sanford has gathered a little company of children, sometimes at the church, sometimes at her own house, according to the weather, and has had with them on Sundays services from the Book of Common Prayer. At a recent visit I confirmed the only member not yet confirmed of a class of little girls whom Mrs. Sanford has kept interested in the Church's attractive and appealing and upbuilding ways for many years, until now they are young ladies. Such a thing as this might be done in many a hamlet in Missouri. Where there's a will, there's a way.

On another visit by the bishop to Jackson, he confirmed four girls who had received instruction from Mrs. Sanford. He remarked that she had received her training in teaching a Sunday School class in St. Louis from W.H. Thomson, a well-known churchman. The bishop greatly admired her zeal and wisdom. He stated that "Jackson can show what, under God's blessing, one earnest and intelligent Church woman can accomplish even in places where no Church services can be kept up." According to Martha Vandivort, in addition to caring for the children of the Episcopal Church, which was on the corner of Mary and First East, Mattie also frequently walked to the church to care for the flowers.

The Bishop also says about Mattie:

At Jackson I baptized a babe, Linus Sanford, great-grandson of her [Mary Frizel Russell] by whose kindness the beautiful lot, on which the beautiful Church of the Redeemer stands, was given to the Church. I confirmed one young lady. She is the last to be confirmed of a class of several who, as little children, used to gather in Mrs. Sanford's home on Sundays to be taught the catechism by Mrs. Sanford long before there was any place of worship of our Church in Jackson. So is the Kingdom like as though one should cast seed into the ground!

Finally came the sad note about the storm that destroyed the church in February of 1924:

A cyclone tore through JACKSON in the month of March, stripped off the roof of our beautiful church, pulled down the bricks, twisted the building out of shape and left a sad and sorry sight. Dear Mrs. Linus Sanford has herself, single-handed, trained many persons in the little Sunday School at Jackson, who have scattered in many directions and have helped to maintain churches in many places. Thanks be to God for this devoted servant of her Master and for her patient, zealous missionary labors.

The Cape Girardeau County Home Comers

In 1908, at seventy years of age, the Honorable Linus Sanford was asked to speak at the first reunion of the Cape Girardeau County Home Coming, at which time the new $90,000 courthouse was dedicated. The subject of his speech, which was printed in *The Jackson Herald*, was "coming back to one's home—the land of one's childhood." Articles and advertisements in *The Jackson Herald* leading up to the event predicted that "this will be the most important and the best attended event that has ever occurred in the history of our city." Citizens were encouraged to donate liberally to defray the expenses. Since such a large crowd was expected, all the hotel accommodations would be filled to capacity. Therefore, the citizens were asked to open their homes to visitors for lodging and even meals if possible. Further, the residents were asked to clean up around their premises: cutting weeds, removing rubbish, whitewashing houses and fences,

Home Coming and dedication of the new courthouse, Jackson, Missouri, September 1908. *Photo courtesy of Jackson Heritage Association.*

and decorating homes and businesses with flags and bunting, which were available for purchase from the merchants.

After the opening speech by Linus for the courthouse dedication, a large variety of events took place. The Sixth Regiment of the National Guard of Missouri held its encampment at Jackson during that week with 9 companies of 450 men leading a soldier's life in camp, including parades, marches, and target practice. The "famous" regiment band—which according to the newspaper played at the Confederate Reunion at Birmingham, Alabama, the summer before—gave several concerts. There were baseball games between the regiment and Jackson as well as between Jackson and the Cape Girardeau Capahas. Other events included a balloon ascension and parachute leap, a grand flower parade, an old fiddlers' contest, a street fair, and carnival show. The courthouse featured an exhibition of historic relics and curios. Of course, no gathering would be complete without a political speech. Both the Honorable W.S. Cowherd, Democratic candidate for governor, and the Honorable H.S. Hadley, the Republican candidate, spoke.

Some interesting contests and prizes were a part of the homecoming:

Oldest woman born in Cape Girardeau County—Prize—Gold-headed umbrella: $6

Oldest man born in Cape Girardeau County—Prize—Gold-headed cane: $6

Oldest woman—Gold thimble

Oldest man—Parker fountain pen: $2.75

Person coming farthest—Gold medal: $5

Largest family—Barrel of Gold Leaf flour

The man and wife married in Cape Girardeau County for the longest date and still living in the county each received a pair of gold-filled spectacles, the lenses of which would be fitted by S.M. Strain, Optometrist. An ad for Mr. Strain in the same newspaper stated that he was "thoroughly educated in the science of reflection and has his office well equipped for any test necessary to the perfect fitting of glasses." In addition, he listed a number of his clients for a reference, including Dr. Henderson and Mayor Russell.

After the event, the October 1 issue of *The Jackson Herald* called the celebration one of the greatest events of this county and estimated the number present on Saturday to be about ten thousand. The event was originally scheduled for August 27–28, but changed to September 24–26 to accommodate the Sixth Regiment to be in attendance. However, after 1908 the Home Coming Reunion would

Mattie and Linus Sanford. *Photos courtesy of Cape River Heritage Museum.*

be scheduled the last week in August.

The Death of Mattie and Linus

The Honorable Linus Sanford died on Saturday, May 18, 1912, in his home in Jackson at the age of seventy-three years, four months, and seventeen days. According to his obituary in the May 23 edition of *The Cash-Book Journal,* he had been in poor health for several years from "chronic stomach trouble," but was confined to his bed only about ten days before his death. He continued his interest in law all of his life, finding pleasure as he grew older reading his law books even when he no longer practiced law. The obituary goes on to note:

> Linus Sanford was a kindly man and a perfect gentleman of the old school. He was sympathetic in his nature and kind and generous to the needy. His family life was most exemplary and his true nature was shown there. To his beloved companion he was always as gentlemanly and as courteous as would be expected of a true gentleman in the presence of any lady.

The funeral was held at the Sanford home at 3:00 P.M. on Monday, May 20, with most of the lawyers of the county in attendance. The services were conducted by the Rev. Charles Maltas, pastor of the Cape Girardeau Episcopal Church. The Episcopalian newspaper *The Church News* quotes the bishop: "Jackson has suffered a severe loss in the recent death of Mr. Linus Sanford, Warder of the Church of the Redeemer, an earnest, faithful man."

From the *Southeast Missourian* newspaper, we learn of the death of Mattie Russell Sanford on March 5, 1927, at the age of eighty years, seven months, and thirteen days. The obituary tells of her death at 4:00 in the morning at the home of her daughter, Mrs. C. S. Vandivort, in Cape Girardeau. Mattie died of pneumonia after being seriously ill for about ten days. She was born at the home of her great-grandfather, George Frederick Bollinger, in Burfordville on July 22, 1846. Her parents were Joseph W. and Mary Frizel Russell. She was the widow of Linus Sanford, who died on May 18, 1912.

Mattie was survived by her son Linus Sanford of Cape Girardeau and two daughters, Julia S. Vandivort of Cape Girardeau and Mattie S. Soderstrom of Benton, Illinois. She also had nine grandchildren. Her body was taken to the Sanford Home in Jackson where the funeral service was held by the Right Reverend Frederick F. Johnson, of St. Louis, Bishop of Missouri, after which she was laid to rest beside Linus in the old city cemetery in Jackson.

As noted, the funerals of both Linus and Mattie were held in the

Mattie and Linus Sanford with grandchildren Russell Sanford Peterman, Mary Vandivort, and Linus Sanford II. *Photo courtesy of Jackson Heritage Association.*

family home. In those days, friends and family would come to the house for the viewing of the deceased, who would be displayed in the parlor, thus the name "funeral parlor." I remember my grandmother's funeral in rural Mississippi when I was seven years old. Her body in her casket was in the parlor, and many neighbors and relatives came to visit, bringing food for the family and visitors. For the night before the funeral, the men of the community signed up for times to sit with the corpse overnight. The funeral was held there in the home the next day with a local gospel quartet and a minister presiding over the ceremony. After the Civil War, the process of embalming became common, and the visitation was gradually moved from the private home to a more neutral setting in a funeral home or parlor.

In reading the obituaries of Lilla and William H. Harrison, who bought Julia's house on Themis Street after her death, I found that both of their funerals were held at 313 Themis. Lilla died at St. Francis Hospital of complications of malaria on September 1, 1920, with the funeral being conducted at the home by the Reverend Morton of the Presbyterian Church on September 3 at 2:00 P.M. William died the next year on August 3, 1921, of a stroke while eating breakfast. His funeral was also conducted at the Themis Street home at 2:00 P.M., Friday, August 5. The Harrisons were laid to rest in the family mausoleum in New Lorimier Cemetery.

Another funeral custom of the nineteenth and early twentieth centuries was wearing black to honor the deceased. The Victorians had a set of strict rules about mourning. For example, a widow was expected to mourn her husband for at least two years, wearing only black made from a dull fabric such as crepe and no jewelry for the first year of "deep" mourning, trading her crepe for black silk and black jewelry for the second year. After that time, the widow could wear any color, although many followed the lead of Queen Victoria, who wore black the rest of her life after the death of her beloved Prince Albert. According to Mattie's granddaughter Julia Stein, Mattie mourned Linus the rest of her life by wearing black.

Julia Stein remembered other traits of her grandmother. She said Mattie was loved by all who came to know her, she had a strong religious belief in the afterlife, and she thought only silver was a satisfactory gift. One of the gifts Mattie treasured was a copy of *Poetical Works of Alfred Tennyson*, which was a Christmas gift in 1862, given to Mattie by her Uncle Charles, her father's half-brother who administered the trust left to her.

At a family reunion, Julia Vandivort Stein shared this family story about her grandparents.

The last part of the married life of Linus and Mattie, they lived on the old home place raising their daughter's son Tump—and enjoying our family who lived across the street. When you remember them, remember he was tall at about 6 feet and she was small at about 5 feet. They looked like an unlikely couple, but they were a devoted couple. Because they had spent their lives in that community, they knew many people and were not lonely.

After Mattie's death, the Sanford Home was unoccupied for a period of time. On April 8, 1895, the city purchased land adjoining the Sanford Home with plans for a city park. However, at that time there were no funds, labor, or equipment to develop the park. The city of Jackson purchased the historical home and seven acres of wooded land in 1933, the funds for the purchase and renovations provided by the WPA. On December 5, the property was bought for $5,000: $3,000 paid, and two notes at $1,000 each. The dense undergrowth was cleared, and a swimming pool, a rock garden, and a low water bridge constructed. A January 1935 article in the *Missouri Magazine* describes the property, which had been developed into a club house and community center with the renovations to the residence and grounds in keeping with the colonial estate. The home was furnished to be used for club meetings, social occasions, and other community events, as well as a home for the caretaker. In 1946, there were two upstairs apartments. The grounds had been artistically landscaped with an athletic field, tennis courts, areas for picnics, and beautiful walkways.

The home is described as presenting a "true southern hospitality" to its notable visitors from abroad, as well as three of the Episcopal bishops from the St. Louis Diocese who stayed with the Sanfords when visiting that part of the state. The story went on to say:

Gay and colorful were the lawn fetes and house parties of the period, when the young ladies of Jackson, in frilled organdies and picture hats thronged the rooms and broad porches of the mansion or strolled with their escorts upon the shaded lawns. And it was the custom of the times for the young men of the social elite to honor the ladies with a return fete—and here again the hospitable Sanford home served its guests right royally. In summer and in winter, the boys and girls of Jackson were always welcomed and freely used the woodland and winding stream of the estate as a happy playground.

Unfortunately, about 1950, when the Jackson City Park was expanded, the home was razed.

Margaret Henderson of Jackson published in *Bard* the following poem about the old Mansion:

BRAVE OLD HOUSE
Brave old house! Within your crumbling walls
The ghosts of ancient glories walk, and sweep
Their skirts of silk that rustle in the still,
Chill silence of your musty sleep.
Wake not to mourn your fallen state
Of sad decay; unmindful, slumber long,
Happy in the shining dreams that fill
Your empty halls with silent, splendid song.

The Sanford Mansion. *Photo courtesy of Jackson Heritage Association.*

Julia and Samuel Harris

Harris

Samuel Stanhope Harris

married

Julia Elizabeth Russell

Born to Samuel and Julia

Stanhope Frizel Harris   Hope Mattie Harris

I was first introduced to Julia E. Harris from a flyer given to Bob and me by the real estate agent when we toured 313 Themis in June of 2003. The article was mostly about Dr. Samuel S. Harris, her husband, and concluded with only two sentences that referred to Julia. "Dr. Harris afterward married Julia Russell. They had two children, both of whom are dead." I have since found out that there is much, much more to know about Julia.

According to family rumors, Julia's earlier planned elopement was thwarted by her family. Later, on January 28, 1880, Julia was married to Dr. Samuel S. Harris. He was born in Jackson, Missouri, on December 25, 1836, the son of Dr. E.W. and Mary Alexander Harris, both natives of North Carolina. Samuel received his medical training at Bellevue Medical College in New York City. After graduating in 1858, he worked at the Bellevue Hospital for two years, returning to Jackson in 1861 to practice medicine for a few months. Upon the beginning of the Civil War, Samuel left his practice and became a renowned officer as he fought with the Confederates. After the war, he resumed his medical practice in Water Valley, Mississippi, later returning to Missouri where he married Amanda Brown, daughter of Missouri Lieutenant Governor Wilson Brown, in 1866. She died in 1867, having borne a daughter, Mary Amanda, who was thirteen years of age when Samuel and Julia were married.

Dr. Harris settled in Cape Girardeau in 1878 and practiced medicine, also becoming the Cape Girardeau postmaster in 1886. An advertisement for his medical services appearing in the *Cape Girardeau Democrat* states that the doctor paid special attention to surgery and diseases of females. His office was located in the rear of Trickey's Drug Store at the corner of Independence and Spanish. An interesting story is connected with him about the naming of Daisy, Missouri. The village was first named Drum Town after the German emigrant, William Drum, who located there before the Civil War. About 1886, the community began to expand with the addition of a new mercantile store, and residents petitioned for a post office. Chapman Kinder, along with Dr. S.S. Harris, began a successful campaign to rename the settlement with its new post office, Daisy—the name of the last baby that Dr. Harris delivered.

The doctor apparently had other interests, also. The *Cash Book Journal*, October 6, 1881, states that "the Doctor says his stave and heading factory in Cape is doing a good business." Staves and headings were used for making wooden barrels, which were in high demand for shipping in the 1800s and early 1900s. Harris's interest in literature led him to contribute his writings to numerous medical journals as well as magazines and newspapers.

According to a note in the March 27, 1897, *Cape Girardeau Democrat*, Samuel Harris's friends decided to circulate a petition to put his name before the people of Cape Girardeau as a candidate on the reform ticket for mayor, even though he did not want to run for mayor. However, since his friends had persevered in getting his name on the ballot, he wrote in the newspaper article that he expected his friends to vote for him. He was described as

a plain every day man. He belongs to no factions. He is a Christian gentleman with no strings tied to him. He belongs to no church—no select organization. He is Dr. Harris—a man who is known far and near for his good qualities. He is the friend of the poor and needy and has always answered the calls of those who suffered with the prangs [*sic*] the human race is subject to whether they had money or not—whether they were dressed in rags or silks. Than Dr. Harris there is no man in the city who is better posted in city affairs what the city needs, and we all know that he has the back-bone and the courage to administer the laws as the law says they shall be administered.

However, despite this flowery endorsement, Harris lost the race to the Democratic ticket.

Christ Episcopal Church Records

Christ Episcopal Church most graciously allowed me to research old church records of members, baptisms, marriages, births, and deaths. Upon turning one page in the birth section, I came upon two names which jumped out at me. They were the babies of Julia and Samuel Harris. As I read *Hope Mattie Harris, born December 16, 1880, and baptized February 20, 1881,* and *Stanhope Frizel Harris, baptized October 22 ,1882,* I felt tears cloud my eyes. I was just imagining how it must have grieved Julia and Samuel to lose both of these babies, who were named for family members: Hope and Stanhope for their father, Samuel Stanhope; Hope for her Aunt Martha Jane "Mattie" Russell Sanford; and Stanhope for the Frizel family of his grandmother, Mary Frizel Russell. The sponsors for Hope's baptism were Mrs. Russell, Mrs. Rucker, and C.F. Robertson. The sponsors for Stanhope were S.S. Harris, Mrs. Mary L. Russell, and Mrs. Martha J. Sanford. The New Lorimier Cemetery Book indicates that in Section one, Lot 124, there are four graves: S.S. Harris (Dr.), date of birth December 15, 1837, death December 6, 1897; Julia E. Russell Harris, date of birth October 10, 1848, death February 2, 1903; S.F. Harris (Stanhope Frizel), date of birth October 22, 1882, death October 30, 1884; but record of the fourth grave shows only a question mark. It has to be the grave of Hope Mattie Russell. Although there are grave markers for Julia and Samuel, there are no markers for the children.

Apparently Stanhope was two when he died, but available records do not indicate when Hope died. However, notes in the *Cash Book Journal* indicate that Dr. Harris and his family visited in Jackson on July 21, 1881, and again on October 6, 1881. The next note on March 23, 1882, says only "Dr. S.S. Harris and lady of the Cape spent Saturday in Jackson." So perhaps Hope had died sometime between October of 1881 and March 23, 1882.

The Building of the House at 313 Themis

Julia, her mother Mary L. Russell, her sister Martha Jane "Mattie" Russell, and her brother James W. Russell had received substantial inheritances after the death of their father Joseph Russell. At the time of Joseph's death, T. Gustine Russell, Charles S. Russell,

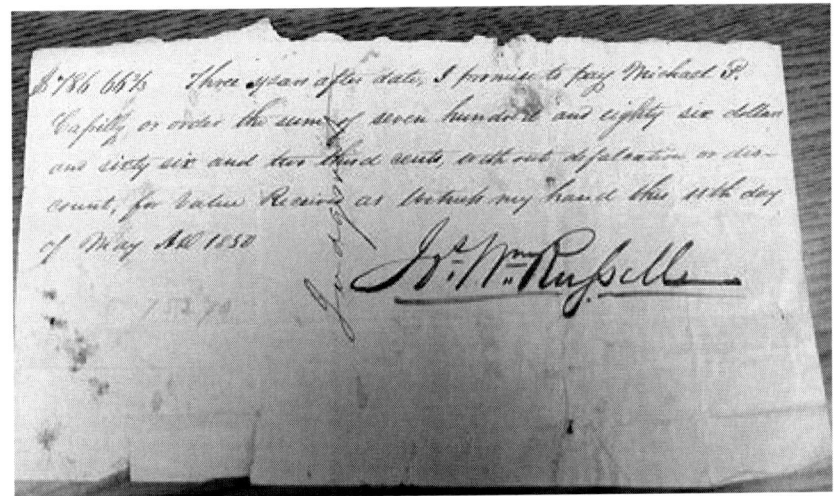

Promissory note signed by Joseph Russell to Michael P. Cassilly on May 11, 1850, for the west one-fourth of Lot 8, Range C, on which Julia Russell Harris's house would be built in 1897–98. *Document courtesy of Cape Girardeau County Archives.*

and George W. Parker were appointed trustees of the children's inheritance. One of the properties that was passed to the family was the west half of Lot 8, Range C, now 313 Themis Street. On my first visit to the Cape Girardeau County Archives, I was handed white gloves along with the probate folder for Joseph Russell and was amazed when I found the original promissory note to buy the property that was signed in large letters by Joseph, dated May 11, 1850, promising to pay Michael P. Cassilly $786.66 2/3 [gold value] in three years for the west one-fourth of the lot. Joseph was the "last and best bidder" at $101 on the other one-fourth at a sale by the sheriff of land owned by Edward B. Cassilly on November 27, 1850. According to the abstract of 313 Themis, on June 4, 1881, "Mary L. Russell widow, James W. Russell and Annie Russell his wife, Sam S. Harris and Julia E. Harris his wife and George W. Parker trustee for Julia E. Harris in consideration of $2,400 conveyed to Martha J. Sanford, 'a part of Lot No. 8 in range C in the City of Cape Girardeau, being the west-half of Lot No. Eight. Being all the real estate owned by the late Joseph W. Russell at the time of his death in this lot . . .'" The next entry in the abstract shows Julia's purchase of the property. "On the 21st day of November 1894 Martha J. Sanford and Linus Sanford her husband, and T. Gustine Russell and Charles S. Russell as Trustees for Martha J. Sanford . . . in consideration of

$1,200 conveyed to Julia E. Harris, all of the west half of Lot No. Eight (8), in range 'C' of the City of Cape Girardeau fronting 94 feet on Themis Street and running back the full depth of said lot 231 feet . . ." The Harrises' new house on this property was begun in May 1897 and completed in 1898.

As my husband Bob and I began to try to delve into the history of this house while doing research to place the house on the National Register of Historic Places, we found articles in the *Cape Girardeau Democrat* about the building of the house. According to the May 8, 1897 issue, Dr. Harris had let the contract to Matthew Doll for "a nice residence building on Themis Street." Henry Koch was to do the brick work. Another report on the house was found in the *Cape Girardeau Democrat* Saturday, August 14, 1897. Henry Koch had completed the brick work and received praise as building one of the finest houses in the city. According to the architect, Jerome B. Legg of St. Louis, "Mr. Koch's idea of mortar and finishing is all right in the construction of this building. It beats the finishing used in any other house in the city."

The Death of Samuel

Unfortunately, Dr. Harris died in St. Luke's Hospital in St. Louis on December 6, 1897, before the house was completed. Christ Episcopal Church records list his death due to liver trouble and dropsy. His remains were returned to Cape Girardeau for the funeral, which was held at the home on Spanish Street. According to the *Democrat*, "It was the largest funeral in the city for many years. The friends of Dr. Harris were legion and they followed the remains of their departed friend to their resting place," which was in New Lorimier Cemetery.

After Samuel's death, Julia presented a petition that was filed on May 23, 1898, requesting that no letters of administration be filed on Samuel's estate. She states that

Samuel Stanhope Harris, husband of Julia Russell Harris. *Photo courtesy* Encyclopedia of the History of Missouri.

he departed this life on the 6th day of December A.D. 1897. That he left the petitioner his widow; that he left no minor children under the age of 16 years. That said deceased left no real estate. That he left no notes or accounts, so far as your petitioner has been able to discover. That he had 25 to 30 volumes of books, those mostly books given by the government and of trifling value. A few surgical instruments of little value and wearing apparel. No other personal property. That all of said effects were not worth two hundred dollars, that there was no cash on hand. Wherefore she prays that no administration be granted on said estate, and that she be allowed to dispose of said effects as she may deem fit, and collect notes and accounts if any may be discovered and for other orders or direction as the court may deem fit.

Julia E. Harris
Widow of Samuel S. Harris
Submitted and sworn to before me this 11th day of February 1898
John F. Woody Notary Public

One thing we couldn't find in our initial research was whether Julia ever lived in the new house, since her husband died while it was still under construction. Our niece helped us locate her in the 1900 census records, but it gave no address. The probate files had revealed all the real estate, etc., that had been passed to Julia by her parents, Joseph W. and Mary F. Russell.

It was obvious, especially after reading her petition to the court after Samuel's death, that the money to build the house came from Julia's side of the family. The more I found out about Julia, the more sure I was that she was the one who was building the house, she was the one who owned the property at 313 Themis that was inherited from the Russell family, she was the one who rode the steamboats to St. Louis, had property there, and perhaps found the architect, Jerome B. Legg, through her St. Louis connections.

The Architect, Jerome B. Legg

Born in Illinois about 1838, Legg came to St. Louis in 1864 to attend Jones Commercial College. While working as a clerk and bookkeeper for George I. Barnett, called the "dean" of Missouri architecture, Legg was encouraged by Barnett to study architecture in his spare time. He worked for a year in the building trades, becoming the superintendent of projects, and went on to become a famous architect of the time. In 1876, he published *A Home for Everybody in City Suburbs, Village and Country*, aimed at the prospering middle class, the pages of which illustrated the ideal suburban home. There are a number of surviving houses in St. Louis designed by Legg. One of those can be found at 29 Washington Terrace, a gated street in which all the houses are on the National Register. Legg designed and built the home in 1906 for an oil millionaire. By 1878, he had a remarkable list of buildings to his credit in the *Tour of St. Louis.*

Legg remodeled the second state capitol building of Missouri in Jefferson City (1882) and built courthouses in St. Francois County (1885), Ste. Genevieve County (1885), Shelby County (1891), Gasconade County (1899), Mississippi County (1901), and St. Charles County (1903), as well as the Ballard County courthouse in Wickcliffe, Kentucky (1905). The Saint Louis Exposition Music Hall for the 1904 World's Fair, which was Legg's most important St. Louis building, built at a cost of $750,000, was praised as one of the largest and grandest in the nation. The Exposition celebrated the centennial of the Louisiana Purchase.

In 1888, Legg came to Cape Girardeau and left his mark in a number of buildings. First, he began the renovation of the 1854 Common Pleas Courthouse, adding on the east side a full-height triangular pedimented portico with four Tuscan columns topped off with a cupola, thus changing the former Federalist style to Classical Revival. The cupola features a group of three arched windows on each side of the square crown of the building. The features of the 1888 renovation are still there on the bluff overlooking the river, giving to the scene a sense of majesty.

Just down the hill from the courthouse, at the northwest corner of Main and Themis Streets, stood the Sturdivant Bank. Colonel Robert Sturdivant acquired the Third Branch Bank of Missouri in 1866, changing the name. In 1892, the old bank building was torn down and replaced with a building designed by J.B. Legg. It was well known for the large clock which hung over the door of the bank.

In 1897–98, Legg designed the house at 313 Themis Street for Julia and Samuel Harris, and he began the Oliver–Leming house at 740 North Street in 1898–99. Just down the street at 702 North Street, Legg designed a home for George Bennett McBride in 1906. One of the homes Legg designed in Cape Girardeau—the home of

116

Staircase in Julia's house (left) and foyer fireplace (right). *Photos by author.*

Scarab beetle design in stained glass window. *Photo by author.*

E.S. Lilly, 129 South Lorimier Street—was featured in the November 1901 issue of *American Homes*, with engravings of the home from a photograph plus the floor plans. According to the magazine, Mr. Legg

> has had great success in designing this class of buildings for the best people in the country and who hopes through the publication of this and similar designs in *American Homes* to receive inquiries from all who wish to build . . . Such a home requires ample grounds to be at its best, yet it could be easily adapted to a city street where isolated dwellings could be built.

Probably the best-known building designed by Legg in Southeast Missouri is Academic Hall, which has become the symbol of Southeast Missouri State University. It was built between 1903 and 1906. Legg had earlier been the architect for the science and art buildings on campus, completing them in 1902.

As I walk through Julia's house, now our house, that Legg built, I can imagine Julia planning the details that would be included in her new home. At the focal point of the stairway in the foyer there is the large 45" by 78" stained glass window capped by a half-round window on the landing of the second floor. The colorful scarab beetle design in the center, an Egyptian symbol of immortality, is wrapped in an evergreen wreath with red berries. The design is then framed by a mauve border, which is surrounded by a larger border of gold.

On a recent September morning, I walked through the foyer as the ball of the rising sun placed itself directly behind the scarab, saying to me, "Hey, look at this!" It took my breath with its brilliance. The sun started waves in the golden sea of the border while the pieces of white glass sparkled like scores of diamonds. In our eight years in the house, it was the first time I had seen it in full array, just at the peak of the blazing orb. Unfortunately, as a result of the renovation of the outside of the house, somewhere between 1905 and 1908, which added a wraparound porch and balcony on the north and east sides of the house, most of the magnificent window is now hidden from view from the outside and cannot be seen in its entirety.

Matching windows in the bay on the first and second floors on the east side of the house contain the same scarab design, as does the small window in the transom of the front door. The ornamental woodwork decorating the foyer and stairway, the five pocket doors, as well as the floor, were constructed from quarter-sawn oak—the most beautiful wood taken from the heart of the oak tree. The oak woodwork in the dining room, parlor, and library was covered by a previous owner with white paint. Thankfully, the foyer was left with its original look.

The first floor contains four of the five fireplaces in the house, each one with its own unique design. The more formal fireplace in the parlor has Ionic columns which frame an intricate white ceramic tile design of a raised flower garland seeming to flow from classical pitchers on either side, all lined delicately with gold. Just below the mantle and above the ceramic design are carved wooden leaves. The larger fireplace in the foyer is made of red bricks with a pattern of terra cotta egg and dart molding above the mantle. An intricate wooden design provides the trim for the edges of the fireplace. A large mirror graces the woodwork above the library fireplace, which is bordered by small green ceramic tiles. The smaller fireplaces in the dining room, library, and upstairs master bedroom seem to have burned coal. A what-not shelf was built into the side of the bedroom fireplace.

Having studied the designs in the house and having read the detailed listing of Julia's possessions bequeathed to her heirs in her will, I was just sure that having built this beautiful house, she would certainly want to live in it. Then, finally, while glancing through a shelf of books at the county archives, I found a book listing obituaries from the *Cape Girardeau Democrat*. There was her obituary, listed nineteen days after she had died, the tribute confirming that she had indeed lived in the beautiful new house for several years before her death.

Julia Harris's Death

In the February 4, 1903, *Cape Girardeau Democrat* a brief announcement appeared on the locals page that Julia's brother, Dr. James Russell of Bird's Point, had come to Cape Girardeau to attend the funeral of his sister, Mrs. Julia Harris, who had died in St. Louis on February 2. Her funeral, which was held from the Episcopal Church, was delayed due to the train bearing her body to Cape Girardeau being late. Her body was interred in the New Lorimier Cemetery beside her family.

Several days later in the February 21, 1903, *Cape Girardeau Democrat* paper was published the following obituary:

> Mrs. Julia E. Harris, the announcement of whose death in
> St. Louis on February 2nd, came with great surprise to many

friends in this county, was the daughter of Joseph William Russell and Mary Frizzel Russell, both of which families were for many years identified with the growth of this section of the country.

Mrs. Harris was born at Jackson, Mo, on October 10, 1848. Her father, Joseph Russell, was a college graduate and a civil engineer of some prominence who located some of the first railroads in the state of Illinois. He came of a patriotic American family which early settled in this country, some of whom came from England and some from Ireland. He was born in Virginia and came west with his parents in infancy. Among his other enterprises he published the first newspaper published in Jackson, Mo.

Mary Frizzell Russell, mother of the deceased, was a granddaughter of George F. Bollinger on her maternal side, who was identified for many years with the early development of Southeast Missouri and a member of the legislature, and a leading and active citizen in all matters concerning the general prosperity.

Through her father's family Mrs. Harris' ancestry is traceable to very old English families, among them the Vance and Pemberton families.

The deceased Julia E. Russell was married to the late Dr. Samuel Stanhope Harris, January 29, 1880, and they made their home in the city of Cape Girardeau until the doctor's death a few years ago. They had two children who died in infancy. Just shortly before the doctor's death a handsome residence was erected by them on Themis street, in Cape Girardeau, but which unfortunately was never occupied by them together, the doctor having died a short while before its completion. After the doctor's death Mrs. Harris lived for several years in the new residence, and afterwards made her home with her sister, Mrs. Sanford, in Jackson, and was living temporarily in St. Louis when she died.

She was a devoted wife and mother and the reverence in which she held the memory of her husband was known to all her friends. She was confirmed by Bishop Robertson in early girlhood and was a communicant and constant worker in the Episcopal Church, in which faith she lived, died and was interred.

Her remains were brought from St. Louis and interred in

Lorimier cemetery on Wednesday, February 4th, the funeral being conducted by the Rev. Mr. Cornell, of St. Louis. She was a woman of strong character, affectionate among her friends, bright and intelligent, and she will be greatly missed by all.

She leaves a handsome estate which she inherited from her father and mother, consisting of real estate in St. Louis, Cape Girardeau, Bird's Point and Alexander county, Illinois, together with some personal property, which was fairly distributed by her will among her next of kin, in addition to substantially remembering her stepdaughter, Mary Harris Blomeyer, wife of Mr. E.F. Blomeyer. Her next of kin consist of Mrs. Martha Sanford, wife of Hon. Linus Sanford, of Jackson, Mo., and their three children, Linus Sanford, Jr., Julia Sanford and Martha Sanford Peterman, and her brother, Dr. James Russell, of Bird's Point, Mo., and his children.

Mr. Frank E. Burrough is made executor of the will and trustee of the property going to Mrs. Peterman.

Although no name was given for the writer of the tribute, I feel that it was possibly done by Miss May Greene, who lived just across from Julia on the corner of Themis Street and attended the Christ Episcopal Church together with Julia on the next corner. Her signature as a witness is on Julia's original will and appears again after Julia's death on her death certificate. Miss Greene and her family were originally residents of Bollinger County but fled to Cape Girardeau during the Civil War to escape persecution due to their allegiance to the Union. She was a beloved teacher of thousands of Cape's children. She taught in the Cape Girardeau schools from 1870, beginning her work in Old Lorimier School and ending as principal of Washington School in 1932. In 1921, the

Graves of Samuel, Julia, Hope, and Stanhope Harris. *Photo by author.*

city named its newest school May Greene School in honor of Miss Greene.

On the same page of the *Cape Girardeau Democrat* as the tribute was a resolution adopted by the Christ Church Guild expressing their sorrow at Julia's passing.

> At the regular meeting of Christ Church Guild a communication was formed to express our deep sorrow at the death of Mrs. Julia E. Harris. God in His all-wise providence has called Mrs. Julia E. Harris from our midst. She was a conscientious, good worker in the church and guild for over twenty years. May our loss be her eternal gain. The deepest affliction of death is not for those who die, but for those who sorrow. Human sympathy is inadequate for the consolation of those who suffer from the bereavement. The hackneyed commonplace utterances on such occasions stir the soul as little as the sable plumes and crepe which custom has presented for the funeral procession. We extend to her relatives our heartfelt sympathy. God grant them in His infinite mercy the feeling that "He doeth all things well."
>
> Mrs. R.L. Wilson
> Mrs. F.E. Burrough
> Mrs. A. Rader
> Mrs. R.C. Dennis

Julia's probate file at the Cape Girardeau County Archives revealed many aspects of her life. Bills dealing with Julia's last days and funeral arrangements showed that she died in St. Louis, attended by Dr. Robert C. Atkinson, who submitted a bill for $25 for her last illness, and Dr. Jim Melvin, who submitted a bill for $6 for two visits. Wagoner Undertaking Company of St. Louis made the arrangements, providing five black, cloth-covered draped cedar burial casket trimmings and box, an engraved name plate, and embalming, as well as taking the remains to the depot, for the total of $298. Apparently the train to Cape Girardeau was late, thus delaying the funeral. The train was met by a hearse to bear Julia to her final resting place beside her husband Samuel Harris in New Lorimier Cemetery, with the hearse being followed by ten carriages, two hacks, and eight surreys which were rented for the occasion. According to the funeral traditions of the period, as mentioned above in the Christ Church Guild tribute, the horses would have had sable plumes attached to the harnesses with their backs draped in black crepe. Finally, there was a statement in the folder from Jackson Marble Works for a granite monument and two granite markers for the graves of the Harrises at a charge of $270.

Julia's family had many ties to the Oak Hill area of St. Louis. An important one was the Holy Innocents Episcopal Church located at Tholazan and Morganford Road near the coal mines area. As the first church located in that area, it was founded in 1871. The original articles founding the church include the names of Charles S. Russell, Russella L. Parker, T.G. Russell, Julia A. Russell, and Mary E. Russell. Julia Elizabeth Russell was baptized by the Reverend A.F. Samuels at the Church of the Holy Innocents on March 10, 1872; her sponsors were Charles S. Russell and Mrs. Russella Lucy Parker, her half-uncle and half-aunt, children of James and Lucy Russell. Julia was soon thereafter confirmed by the Right Reverend Charles Franklin Robertson, the second bishop of the Diocese of Missouri, on June 16, 1872, in Jackson. This is recorded in the bishop's journal, which is on deposit at the Diocese Archives for the Episcopal Church in St. Louis. The Reverend Frederick W. Cornell was rector of Holy Innocents from 1896–1900. When Julia died in St. Louis on February 2, 1903, he accompanied her body to Cape Girardeau and presided over her funeral. As the coal diggings disappeared in the early part of the twentieth century, the church also declined, closing its doors in 1935.

Julia's Generous Will to Her Family

Julia's will, signed and dated September 5, 1899, covered an amazing fortune that included properties in St. Louis; Cape Girardeau; Mississippi County, Missouri; and Alexander County, Illinois. She expressed her strong faith in the opening of her will: "I will my soul to God, who gave it, trusting in a joyful resurrection in the life to come."

The heirlooms bequeathed to family members present a review of historical ancestors of the family and the treasures they left to be passed down the generations.

In Julia's words,

> I bequeathe to my nephew Linus Sanford (Junior), one dozen solid silver tablespoons, marked "J.E.R." [Julia Elizabeth Russell]. Ten solid silver teaspoons marked "M.L.R." [Mary Langdon Russell]. Solid silver spoon and fork marked "S.F.H." [Most likely the child-size silverware which belonged to Stan-

hope Frizel Harris, the son of the Harrises who died at age two.] Silver soup terreen [*sic*] marked "J.E.R." Silver crumb tray and scraper. A teal blood-stone ring that belonged to my father [Joseph Russell]. My gold watch, marked, "J.E.R." A crayon picture "Ariadne." One oil painting—"Lake Lucia." One water color painting by my mother [Mary Russell]. An ivory rule and compass, owned by my father. [Joseph Russell, who would have used the tools as an engineer.] A wooden rule owned by grandfather [Joseph] Frizel. Masonic apron and sack. [Most likely belonging to Joseph Frizel since he was one of the organizers of the Masons in Jackson.] And an old gun that belonged to grandfather [James] Russell.

Next, she made her bequest to her niece Julia Adele Sanford:

One set of Emerald jewelry (two long pieces and one ring) which was left by my mother with the direction that the same should be given by me to Julia. [Later Julia Adele Sanford Vandivort had the emeralds made into rings for her daughters and daughters-in-law.] Also, one set cameo jewelry. One dozen solid silver dinner forks marked "J.E.H" [Julia Elizabeth Harris]. One dozen solid silver after dinner coffee spoons, marked "J.E.H." One dozen dinner knives, pearl handles. An oil painting—"Blacksmith Shop." Oil painting— "Theodosia Burr." An oil painting of my late husband, Dr. Samuel S. Harris. Small water color painting "Pomegranates," by grandma Daugherty. Small work box, which was a bridal present to Grandma Frizel, together with its contents, excepting a small odd vinaigrette, which I bequeathe to her sister Mattie. Also, to Julia my lace box, containing lace and other articles, except four pieces marked. Also, a silver tea set of five pieces and dish. Also ½ dozen tea spoons.

To her sister Mattie Russell Sanford, Julia willed:

one solid silver porringer [a small dish for porridge], one solid silver fork, and two solid silver tablespoons known in the family as Frizel silver. One solid silver napkin ring, my decorated china set, and all other china not herein otherwise mentioned. Also glassware, table linen, bedding and wearing apparel, not otherwise bequeathed. Also, a framed photograph of my father, with dog.

Julia bequeathed to her niece Mattie Sanford:

> One dozen solid silver dessert forks, marked "J.E.R." One half dozen solid silver teaspoons, marked "J.E.R." One solid silver cup marked "S. Frizel Harris." [This would have been a child-sized cup belonging to Stanhope Harris.] One dozen pearl-handled dessert knives. Silver pitcher waiter and goblet. Silver card receiver. Garnet stick pin. My gold chain for a watch. Oil painting of St. John. Oil painting, "Farm Scene." Water color painting by my mother. Work box owned by my mother. An old fan owned by Grandma Frizel. An oil painting—"Buttermilk Waterfall." Also, a piece of lace worked for her.

Family treasures left to Julia's nieces, Annie and Lizzie Russell, daughters of her brother James, were:

> [To Annie] a solid silver butter knife marked "J.E.R." Solid silver salt spoon marked "R." Silver cheese spoon. Silver butter dish. Silver coster. Silver syrup stand. Crayon picture of my father. One small oil painting 8 x 11. A piece of lace done by my mother.
> [To Lizzie] six or eight solid silver teaspoons marked "J.E.R." One silver fish knife. One silver cake dish marked "M.L.R." Glass and silver pickle stand. Crayon picture of my mother. One small oil painting 7 x 10. One half dozen silver knives. A lace scarf done by my mother.

Her brother was next in the will, receiving some of the family furniture heirlooms. Julia wrote:

> to my brother James W. Russell, Hand painted plate—marked "St. Louis Jockey Club." Chafing dish. Part of my old blue china namely, 1 meat plate, 2 tea plates and one cup and saucer. A set of six china plates in gilt cupids. A Chinese cup, china cup, saucer and cover. Six embroidered finger bowl doileys. Six small embroidered glass doiley's. One heavy bright calico comfort. 4 Linen sheets and two square Feather pillows. One bed room set of walnut furniture, bought when I went to house-keeping, and consisting of bedstead, dresser, and wash-

stand. A rocking chair, and one half dozen cane-seat chairs. An old walnut table that belonged to my mother—(was one half dining table), and the old cherry table that belonged to grandpa Bollinger.

To her step-daughter, Mary A. Harris Blomeyer, Julia bequeathed "one solid silver soup ladle, one solid silver sugar tongs and one sugar spoon. Small oil painting—'Gunboat Arkansas' [which her father served on during the Civil War]. Crayon picture of Dr. E.W. Harris. Two small framed photographs of her father and a little plush box with button, which belonged to her father."

Finally, she came to the real estate property that she owned. Except for a house on Merriwether Street, all the Cape Girardeau properties (including 313 Themis) and her farm in Alexander County, Illinois, as well as her shares of stock at the First National Bank, were left to her nieces and nephew, Mattie, Julia, and Linus Sanford, share and share alike. The Bird's Point property, along with any other property not listed in the will, would go to her sister Mattie Russell Sanford, and at Mattie's death would pass to her three children, Mattie, Julia, and Linus Sanford. Her brother James was to receive the Mississippi County property, which would pass upon his death to his daughters Annie and Lizzie Russell. Julia's house and lot on Merriwether Street in Cape Girardeau was willed to Mary Harris Blomeyer. The St. Louis property left to Julia by her father and mother was to be sold and the proceeds were to pay all final expenses after her death, at which time the balance would be divided, share and share alike, among her nieces, Mattie and Julia Sanford, and her nephew, Linus Sanford.

On April 6, 1903, Linus Sanford Jr. and Julia A. Sanford sold their 2/3

Julia's house. *Photo by author.*

interest in the house and lot at 313 Themis Street to William H. Harrison for $6,000. On April 11, 1903, Mattie Sanford Peterman also sold her 1/3 share to Mr. Harrison for $3,000, which was handled by her trustee Frank Burrough under the restriction written into a codicil to her will by Julia Harris that Mattie's inheritance would be managed by a trustee and that her husband would have no control over her trust. A member of the Harrison family would live in the house for the next eighty-three years. On March 26, 1986, Pam Spradling, a great-granddaughter of the Harrisons, and her husband Albert Spradling sold the house and lot to Dr. Jesse R. Ramsey for $148,000.

Julia Adele and Clyde Vandivort

Vandivort

Clyde Arthur Vandivort

Married

Julia Adele Sanford

Born to Clyde and Julia

Mary Vandivort

Paul Marshall Vandivort

Sanford Russell Vandivort

Charles Alexander Vandivort

Clyde Arthur Vandivort

Julia Sanford Vandivort

Dorothy Virginia Vandivort

Marjorie Adele Vandivort

Patricia Vandivort

Julia Adele Sanford, the daughter of Mattie and Linus Sanford and the niece of Julia Russell Harris, received her education first from tutors and then at Bishop Robertson Hall in St. Louis before going to the New England Conservatory of Music in Boston. Prior to returning to Jackson, Julia taught at the Normal School of the conservatory. As a mother, she taught music to her children.

Julia married Clyde Arthur Vandivort on September 28, 1904, at 8:00 P.M. in the parlor of the old Sanford Mansion on the hill approaching Jackson from the north. The Jackson swimming pool is located there presently. The wedding vows were administered by the Reverend Leslie F. Potter, Archdeacon of Christ Episcopal Church, St. Louis, with Julia's brother and sister, Linus Sanford Jr.

and Martha S. Peterman, serving as witnesses. The newlyweds spent their honeymoon at the World's Fair in St. Louis. When "setting up housekeeping" they first lived at 504 Bellevue Street in Cape Girardeau, later moving to 630 North Street. Nine children were born to the Vandivorts, seven of whom reached adulthood. They were: Mary (b. July 9, 1905–d.July 13, 1976); Clyde Arthur (b. August 22, 1906–d. July 16, 1907); Paul Marshall (b. January 31, 1908–d. December 26, 1977); Julia Sanford (b. August 4, 1909–d. January 29, 2008); Sanford Russell (b. January 17, 1912–d. September 27, 1977); Dorothy Virginia (b. December 25, 1913–d. May 23, 2003); Charles Alexander (b. August 26, 1915–d. November 24, 1982); Patricia (b. September 30, 1917–d. January 11, 1990); and Marjorie Adele (b. May 7, 1920–d. August 15, 1920). A family note suggests that Clyde Arthur died young, perhaps from whooping cough. Paul Stein remembers his grandmother telling about losing a child in a fire, although no mention is made of which child. Another interesting story is about Mary, who was not given a middle name at her "father's insistence to assure that Vandivort would always be her middle name and would survive if she married."

Julia Adele in Public Service

Because of her great interest in children, Julia served as the Cape Girardeau Parent-Teacher Association president from 1922–1926. The first woman to be elected to the Cape Girardeau Board of Education, she served in that capacity for three 3-year terms from 1922–1931. The last two terms, she was elected the vice president of the board.

The headline in the *Southeast Missourian* on March 7, 1922, reads: "WOMEN PLACE 2 CANDIDATES IN THE FIELD— Decide to Oppose Men Running for School Board Place." The news article goes on to say that at a mass meeting of the women of Cape Girardeau on Monday afternoon, Mrs. C.A. (Julia) Vandivort and Mrs. H.J. Houser received the endorsement of the group to run for the Cape Girardeau School Board. Although no organized plan had been made prior to the meeting, the ladies were aware that placing women candidates on the ballot would be proposed. The nominations were made at the end of the gathering when, according to the article, the "question of the women of this city 'dipping' in politics was fully threshed out." Mrs. A.S. Duckworth declared: "I think that it is entirely all right that we have women on the school board and I am also in favor of having at least one candidate for city commissioner."

However, the women decided not to nominate candidates for city commissioner at that time.

After Mrs. Duckworth spoke, a motion was made and passed that candidates for school board be nominated. After the motion passed, Mrs. A.H. Hinchey, who voted against the motion, stated, according to the newspaper, that if she must stand alone, she would do so, because she believed that "the time was not ripe for women to get out for offices."

Two days later at the Washington School Parent-Teacher meeting, new officers were elected, with Julia Vandivort becoming the president. While covering the activities of this meeting, the *Southeast Missourian* printed this announcement:

> The Washington P.-T. Association endorse the nomination of Mrs. C. A. Vandivort and Mrs. H.J. Houser as candidates for members of the School Board at the coming election, not because of opposition to the men, but because we honestly believe this is a place which needs to be filled by the mothers as well as the fathers. First, the mother is constantly studying the needs of the child; second, under certain conditions the teacher feels more free to discuss special problems with the mother; third, the mother more readily sees the little things which need attention and it is the little things that help to form the whole; fourth, throughout the progress of civilization the place of woman has been and is vital to the child's life in the home, in the school and therefore in the directing and guiding of all affairs pertaining to the school the mother's place should be seen readily by all thinking people.

On March 29, 1922, the newspaper noted that two women candidates had tendered their names and that two men were also expected to file for the two 3-year openings on the Cape Girardeau School Board. Apparently there was a last-minute scramble to secure two men to prevent a ballot with only women. Both Mrs. Houser and Mrs. Vandivort declared their support for economy in school administration, with Mrs. Vandivort adding her opposition to the practice of allowing the smaller girls in Central High School to mingle with the older students.

The writer of a "Letter to the Editor" dated March 30, 1922, pointed out that the voters would have their first opportunity to cast a ballot for women. In Illinois, women had been elected for years.

Also pointed out was that "Mrs. House and Mrs. Vandivort are fearless and will regard the opportunity to serve the community at a personal sacrifice as a high honor . . . They will serve the community regardless of creed or color."

The Board of Education

The April 4, 1922 minutes of the Cape Girardeau Board of Education describe the election procedure.

> The Board of Education met at its office in Central High School for the purpose of receiving the returns of the annual school election held April 4, 1922, and for transacting such other business as might come before the Board.
>
> The ballots, poll books, and tally sheets were delivered by the judges of the election, and these were tabulated in the presence of the Board of Education and found to be as follows: School Tax Levy; For 1155–Against 604.

The voters approved the increase in tax from forty cents to one hundred cents of the one hundred dollars assessed valuation. Therefore, the board certified the increase in property tax. The voting places used at that time were interesting: city hall, Vogt Tin Shop, Riverside Lumber Company, Bottling Works, court house, and the Old Hospital.

Next the votes for two school board directors for a three-year term were counted: James A. Kinder, 1,435 votes; Mrs. C.A. Vandivort, 1,230; D.B. Smith, 1,111; and Mrs. H.J. Houser, 1,106. The secretary was instructed to issue certificates of election to Mrs. Vandivort and Mr. Kinder and to notify them of their election. "Woman Is Chosen School Director" was the *Southeast* headline on April 5; thus, Mrs. Vandivort became the first woman elected to office in Cape Girardeau.

According to the Cape Girardeau School Board minutes from her first term, Julia stood up to her promise to practice economy in the administration of the school business. At the April 24 board meeting,

> the matter of granting the superintendent leave of absence during the first half of the school year 1922–23 was discussed, and the board voted to grant the superintendent the privilege of taking leave of absence for a six weeks' term during the summer

on full pay, or as a second alternative, during a six weeks' term during the summer and the first four months of the fall term on half pay. The vote on this proposition was Meyer, Bowman, Kinder, Neal- 'aye,' Mrs. Vandivort, 'no.'

While having the courage to follow through on her campaign promise, she lost her vote this time.

Other business presented was the building committee report recommending that Jefferson School should be remodeled, that Broadway School should have a new roof, new floors and certain changes made in cloak rooms, as well as that the Lorimier School basement should be repaired and that the southwest corner of the study hall should be rebuilt. No definite action was taken on this report.

The president was authorized to appoint a committee of three to appear before the city council to urge that streets and sidewalks be built, leading from Sprigg Street to the May Greene School, which had been completed in 1920.

Reading through the April minutes and reports from the board meeting reveals some of the issues that were being dealt with that would become major issues in the years ahead. The grand total for students in Cape Girardeau in 1922 was 2,181, which included: "White-Male, 1,000, Female, 995; Total, 1,995. Colored-Male, 90;

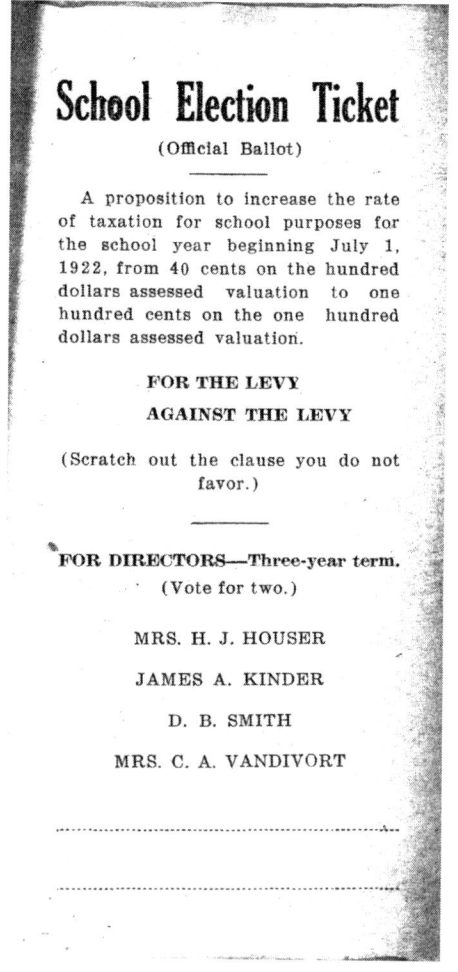

School election ticket. Mrs. C.A. Vandivort was the first woman elected to the Cape Girardeau School Board. *Image courtesy Cape Girardeau Board of Education.*

Old Jefferson School, Cape Girardeau. *Photo by author.*

Female, 96; Total, 186." One of the items of business was the matter of selecting and appropriating funds for the commencement speakers; not one but two, since at that time Cape Girardeau had two high schools: Central High School for the white children and Lincoln High School for the African American children.

Further research revealed that Lincoln was built in 1890. It was later renamed by the board of education in 1925 for John S. Cobb, who served as principal and teacher at the school for thirty-eight years. At the dedication of the building, it was noted: "It was only through hard labor, persistent study and a determined effort that Cobb rose from the ranks of slavery in which he was born to become one of the foremost Negro educators in Missouri. He was an ardent student, conversant with the classics and his personal library was an excellent one."

On March 17, 1953, Cobb School burned (under rather mysterious circumstances that were never fully understood). Only the gymnasium survived the fire. Also lost was the trophy the basketball team had just won three days earlier by claiming the state Negro basketball championship. No immediate plans were made to replace the school due to the anticipated ruling on *Brown vs. Board of Education of Topeka, Kansas*, expected from the Supreme Court to deal with the issue of "separate but equal" population of schools. Another factor was that across town, a new Central High School was under construction on Caruthers, and integration would perhaps be the less expensive solution to the problem. For the remainder of the school year, the black elementary students from Cobb School were transferred to Jefferson School (located at 731 Jefferson Avenue), with the white elementary students from Jefferson transferring to May Greene School. The gymnasium, which was not damaged in the fire, was partitioned into classrooms for the high school students.

On May 17, 1954, the U.S. Supreme Court made its landmark decision declaring segregation unconstitutional; thus, on September 7, 1954, the new Central High School was opened to all students in grades 7–12, thus integrating the Cape Girardeau schools for the first time. Jefferson School was opened as a voluntary school for black elementary students, with other elementary schools available for choice according to the neighborhood in which the child lived. For the first year, the majority of the black elementary children chose Jefferson. Unfortunately, the teachers from the black schools were not hired to continue with the exception of Jefferson School, where the voluntary students were black. In later years, one student who stayed on at Jefferson said she and others did so to protect her teacher's job. In 1955, Clara Daniels became the first African American to graduate from Central High.

Julia and the Episcopal Church

Also important in Julia Vandivort's life was her church. She was a founding member of the small Episcopal Church in Jackson, where her name appears on the list of members applying to the Episcopal Diocese for mission status on July 29, 1903. The mission became Church of the Redeemer on September 18, 1903. The membership roll at the Church of the Redeemer contains the list of Vandivort children and their baptismal dates: Mary, September 17, 1905; Clyde, November 25, 1905; Paul, May 17, 1908; Julia, October 25, 1909; Sanford, Whit Sunday, May 26, 1912; Dorothy, Easter, April 12, 1914; Charles, October 24, 1915; and Patricia, June 23, 1918; plus family weddings and baptisms of grandchildren and other family members. Mary Vandivort had the distinction of being the first person baptized in the new Jackson church. After the storm of 1923, which demolished the church, the Vandivorts became active members of Christ Episcopal Church in Cape.

Historical objects of interest at Christ Episcopal Church are the plaques which hang in the sanctuary. The first contains this quote:

Christ Episcopal Church, Cape Girardeau. *Photo by author.*

"To the Glory of God and in memory of JULIA ADELE SAN-
FORD VANDIVORT 1877–1955 a soul full of grace and beauty
by her faithful devotion a builder and sustainer of this church." On
the opposite side of the sanctuary is a similar plaque honoring Julia's grandmother: "To the glory of God and in memory of MARY
LANGDON FRIZEL RUSSELL 1821–1895 who by her stead-
fast purpose and perseverance made possible the foundation of this
church."

In the minutes of the Christ Episcopal Church Guild are found
glimpses into the mission work Julia was doing in the 1930s, in the
midst of the Great Depression, as she worked with the other ladies
of the church to raise money for causes both in Cape Girardeau and
far away places like Minnesota, Alaska, and Utah. In February 1930,
a series of waffle luncheons were suggested by Helen Batjed to be
served on Tuesdays for six weeks with the luncheons taking the place
of the usual sewing projects. A motion was made by Mrs. Vandivort
(Julia) that waffles, sausages, and coffee be served for a charge of fifty
cents for all that could be eaten; however, Mrs. Harvey moved that
the charge be thirty-five cents, which carried. All materials for the
luncheons would be bought and paid for by the guild. Committees
were appointed by the president to make posters, to call the *Missourian* newspaper, and to make telephone calls. Other jobs assigned
were setting tables, cooking and serving, securing waffle irons and

fuses, washing the dishes, and providing equipment and linen. The president would be allowed one dollar for purchasing cream or syrup pitchers, sugar bowls, and egg beaters. The net amount made on waffle luncheons was $16.74. On February 25, the ladies decided to switch the menu for luncheons to chicken gumbo, coffee, pie, and rice. However, this proved to be too expensive, so the next luncheon menus were chicken and dumplings, slaw, coffee, rolls, jelly, and preserves. The total profit for five luncheons was $50.74.

On January 27, 1931, Julia Vandivort was elected treasurer of the guild. She gave reports on the bonds that the group purchased, such as a $100 school bond which had matured with an interest of $36, bringing the balance of their bank account to $202.97. After some discussion the ladies voted to purchase a $20 industrial loan bond. In the years 1935–36, Julia served as secretary of the group.

In 1931, the guild, which had thirteen members at this time, was asked to help pay half of the expense of the church repairs which would be about $100. The guild voted to inform the vestry that the guild had no available funds; however, if the vestry could take care of the bill, as soon as the guild raised the money, they would pay one-half of the bill. Some of the money-raising projects were boat excursions with Captain Leyhe on one of his several steamboats, which cleared $20, and a bake sale at Bergman's Grocery, which cleared $28.23. In October, the group met in an all-day session to plan the Christmas bazaar, followed by a series of eight more all-day sessions in October through December. By January, they began all-day meetings weekly through April to get ready for the Spring Bazaar. The spring assignment of sewing projects from the Diocese was six muslin night gowns, for children age four years, and six large-size muslin bloomers with a cash allotment of $5 to be sent to the Church of the Holy Spirit (Indian) in Randett, Utah.

In May 1931, Mrs. Hazel Strickler, the daughter of William and Lilla Harrison, announced that, realizing the need of the church for a new organ, she had recently had occasion to inspect some organs while in Chicago and found one best suited to their needs for $500. She further stated that she would pay half the cost if the guild would raise the balance. The ladies enthusiastically approved this generous offer. In the 1934 minutes, the organ resurfaces. Apparently the new organ was purchased, since Mrs. Beardsley reported that the Poplar Bluff people were glad to get the old organ. Mrs. Strickler then asked Mrs. Beardsley to inquire for how much the piano in storage would sell.

In September 1931, a church telephone bill for $1.95 was read and ordered held for investigation. It was later paid. However, in order to save money the group decided that, with the rector's approval, one phone would be taken out and the remaining one put on a party line.

In July 1932, Mrs. Himmelberger made the motion that instead of having bake sales or other affairs through the summer, every woman of the church be asked for free will offerings to the monthly Building and Loan payment for the next two-three months. The motion carried.

In February 1934, two pairs of curtains for the hospital were made with the material being purchased with Eagle Stamps. Several entries note donations to the hospital, which was most likely the newly built Southeast Hospital that had opened in 1928. The hospital was on a "shoestring" budget and had a chicken coop and vegetable garden on the grounds. It relied upon the charity of the community for everything from canned fruit to feather pillows. In the 1930s and 1940s, patients often paid their bills with live chickens or boxes of fresh vegetables. In September, the ladies met and put up sixty-two jars of fruit—apples, pears, and plums—which were to be given to the hospital and the Salvation Army.

Some of the activities reported for the year of 1934 were sewing projects: making dresses for the Red Cross, making over blankets and towels for nursery school, sewing altar linens and collars to be used with vestments at the church, making clothes for children in the Smelterville (in south Cape Girardeau) nursery, and providing clothes for a family of three. Their Diocese assignments were twelve dresses, which were sent to St. Andrews mission in Puerto Rico along with $5, and three dresses sent to the Reverend Mr. Nelson, Grand Rapids, Minnesota. One of their fund raisers was a sale of tickets held for a drawing for a quilt. The ladies also made and filled Christmas bags for Army and Navy men at the Sailors' Hospital. The guild as a body attended a peace meeting in the Presbyterian Church. The church secured a loan on the Parish House to rebuild the church with the new rate being 6 percent against $2,200.

In April 1934, Mrs. Vandivort gave a luncheon for the guild. The Secretary noted: "Mrs. Vandivort served delicious refreshments."

Julia Adele, the Genealogist

Julia Adele Sanford Vandivort was a very enthusiastic genealogist and assembled a trove of family history. Julia's father Linus Sanford had begun researching the family history and passed the torch along to Julia, who kept a very detailed genealogy notebook as she searched for her family. Many of these notations have been listed in the book, *Clyde Arthur and Julia Sanford Vandivort of Cape Girardeau, Missouri, Their Ancestors and Descendants*, compiled by their great-grandson Paul A. Stein. Julia traveled to the East Coast to see firsthand the historical documents and places of her ancestors, taking notes along the way. Typically she not only took notes but also made sure that the statement was certified.

One note made by Julia in Massachusetts reads:

> Richard Silvester, Dorchester, Massachusetts, 18th of October, 1590. [No indication what the date represents, probably birth date.] He was a proprietor of land. From Dorchester he moved to Weymouth, Massachusetts, and was fined tuppence and disfranchised in 1638 for joining an attempt to organize a church which was not authorized by the authorities. He sold out in Weymouth in 1640, and moved to Marshfield where he was for a time a town officer. His wife's name was Naomi. His will was probated on the 24th of September, 1663.

On a different page of information apparently copied in the Newbery, Massachusetts Library, Julia wrote that Richard lived most of his life in Scituate, Massachusetts, in the free colony of Plymouth, in that part now known as Two Mile Creek.

Julia had one page in her journal signed by H.R. McIllwain, State Librarian, Richmond, Virginia, August 14, 1919, in which he certifies that "in the manuscript volume in the Virginia State Library which is referred to as 'Pittsburgh Pay Roll' and which contains the roll of troops paid at Pittsburgh early in the Revolutionary War, there appears on pages 29 and 30 and elsewhere references to payments to Joseph Russell for service in Captain Paul Froman's Company."

Another documentation is certified by Sarah Fulkerson White on March 23, 1931, that her brother, Joseph Russell Fulkerson, owns the Bible of his grandfather Joseph Russell, and this family record is an exact copy from this Bible.

DEATHS
Joseph Russell departed this life May 27, 1817.
Margaret Campbell Russell departed this life March 16, 1822.
BIRTHS
Children of Joseph Russell and Margaret Campbell Russell:

William Russell June 8, 1779
Alexander Russell August 20, 1781
Joseph and Benjamin Russell November 14, 1783
James Russell February 27, 1786
Elizabeth Russell May 27, 1789
Moses Russell November 6, 1792
Mary Russell January 26, 1795
[James Russell is the great grandfather of Mrs. C.A. Vandivort, Cape Girardeau, MO.]

Other journal notes come from the *Encyclopedia of St. Louis History* by Hyde and Conard, Vol. IV, and Houck's *History of Southeast Missouri*, Vol. III, page 61, which tell about James Russell's contributions to Missouri.

Julia was the great-great-granddaughter of Andrew Ramsey and the great-great-great granddaughter of George Frederick Bollinger, who were among the first founders of communities west of the Mississippi River. Thomas Sanford, Julia's six-times great grandfather, came to the Massachusetts Colony in 1630 aboard the "Arbella" with Governor John Winthrop.

Julia was a member of many historical societies, joining the Cape Girardeau Nancy Hunter Chapter of the Daughters of the American Revolution on April 5, 1923, later becoming a regent of the organization. Julia's DAR application shows eleven Revolutionary War ancestors. She became a founder of the Thomas Sanford chapter of Daughters of American Colonists, the chapter named after her ancestor. Julia served as chapter regent of the group as well. Other historical groups in which she held membership were the Confederate Daughters of America, the Ancient and Honorable Artillery Company, and the Colonial Dames Cape Girardeau chapter, of which she was a founding member. In addition, she was involved in organizing a historical society in Cape Girardeau.

The Ancient and Honorable Artillery Company was founded in 1637 by a prominent group of Boston merchants and magistrates in the Massachusetts Bay Colony. It seems to have acquired its name from a similar organization in London. It is the oldest military organization in America, as well as the third oldest in the world. Its members served in the American Revolution, continuing to serve in later wars also. Present day members serve as a ceremonial guard to the governor of Massachusetts at official functions. Descendants from early members of the company may join by right of descent. An auxiliary group for women descendants was formed in 1927, requiring the applicant to be eighteen years or over, lineally descended from a member between the years of 1637–1774, or the descendant of a clergy who preached the annual election sermon during those years.

According to Julia Adele's notes, Ebenezer Pemberton, born to James and Sarah Willey Pemberton on February 3, 1671/72, is listed as the preacher of the sermon for the artillery company on June 1, 1701, and again in 1709, thus qualifying Julia to attain membership in the auxiliary. A graduate of Harvard College, Pemberton served as minister of the Third Church (Old South Church) in Boston from 1700–1717. As noted in Mary Frizel Russell's will, the old Pemberton family Bible was given to her son James Russell.

Because of Julia's interest in genealogy, she and Clyde wanted to preserve the old Bollinger Mill. According to a January 23, 1954, story in the *Southeast Missourian*, Clyde Vandivort offered a start of $1,000 toward buying the old Bollinger Mill and thirteen acres from Cape Girardeau County Milling Company. His idea suggested that property be purchased by Cape Girardeau County, enabling each citizen to feel ownership of the mill. Vandivort felt the mill should be repaired and put to use as a corn mill or a dining lodge furnished in the style of the eighteenth-century period in which it was erected.

Dedication of Bollinger Mill State Park and Burfordville Covered Bridge, July 23, 1961. *Photo courtesy of Jackson Heritage Association.*

Although his idea never developed, later in 1954, Clyde purchased the Bollinger Mill and adjoining twenty-four acres property as a gift for his wife Julia. Their intention was to present it as a gift to the state. Before the proposed gift could be finalized, however, Julia died in February of 1955. The plans were dropped temporarily. After Clyde's death in 1956, Paul Vandivort, the eldest son of the Vandivorts who inherited the property, donated it to the Cape Girardeau County Historical Society for public recreation. On July 23, 1961, the mill property was transferred to the Park Board of Missouri with the exception of a right-of-way for the Bollinger family to access the family cemetery. The preservation of this important piece of Missouri history is a lasting tribute to Julia and Clyde Vandivort and a pleasant setting for summertime folk music concerts, picnics, and visits to the old mill and Bollinger Family Cemetery.

The Vandivort Reunions

In the 1940s, Clyde and Julia Vandivort began a tradition of a family reunion on the Fourth of July, continuing until the present time. Not only is it a time of renewing kinship, but also a time of recalling and sharing the history of the family. Some of the reunion events have included visiting the dungeon in Common Pleas Courthouse where Linus Sanford was imprisoned in the Civil War, seeing the building formerly housing the Sturdivant Bank on the corner of Main Street and Themis where Clyde was president, or attending services at the Christ Episcopal Church. Mary Vandivort DeVaul is quoted in the *Southeast Missourian* about the forty-sixth reunion held in 2003: "I love it because this reunion is arranged so I can learn more each time I come. It really makes a difference to me because I've lived in many places, but I know where I came from."

In 1954, on the fiftieth anniversary of their marriage, Julia and Clyde entertained family and friends at their home on North Street. Every living relative of the Sanford/Vandivort family tried to attend, along with many friends.

Julia Adele's daughter Julia Stein wrote about her mother in the late 1900s.

> She said to me many times, people are the only really important thing. She lived this as her family always came first even if she was involved in some outside activity—as she usually was. All of us can attest to how loving she was and her grandchildren who knew her remember that, too. That she was a very strong

person physically was certainly good. But the main thing was that she was very loving and beloved.

About her father, Julia remembered that Clyde felt very strongly that his daughters should learn accounting and some business in order to be able to manage their own affairs.

The Women of Bollinger and Women's Rights

Several years after we bought Julia's house, I discovered Julia's will, along with a codicil to the will, in the 1903 abstract prepared for the house when it was sold after Julia's death. Since Julia's niece Mattie Sanford Peterman, who would be one of her heirs, had married Berne S. Peterman on June 4, 1901, Julia had added on January 14, 1902, the codicil to her previous will, setting up a trust that would include the real estate and bank stock that Mattie would inherit from Julia's estate. The trustee, Frank E. Burrough, would have the power to re-invest, lease and collect profits, and pay taxes and expenses, paying the annual returns to Mattie Sanford Peterman during her natural life. The trust would be free from any interest or control of her husband. I was surprised to learn of this sort of protection for women being written into a will dated 1902. When I read Mary Frizel's will, I found that she also included this protection for her female heirs, so I did some research to find the status of women's rights in the 1800s.

The Timeline of Legal History of Women in the United States shows that in 1769, the American colonies based the legal status of married women on the English common law which is: "By marriage the husband and wife are one person in the law. The very being and legal existence of the woman is suspended during the marriage, or at least incorporated into that of her husband under whose wing and protection she performs everything." In 1777, laws were passed by all the colonies that took away a woman's right to vote.

In 1839, Mississippi became the first state to grant women the right to hold property in their own name—with a stipulation that the woman have the husband's permission. New York followed in 1848 with a Married Women's Property Act, which granted married women some control over their property and earnings. The act covered women who were single but might marry, as well as women who were already married in 1848. Any of a woman's real and personal property presently owned or any that she would later acquire by rents, issues, profits, gift, grant, devise, or bequest would not be subject to

Clyde and Julia Vandivort with grandchildren. *Photo courtesy of Clyde Vandivort and Paul Stein.*

Summer 1950

Summer 1950 Vandivort family reunion. *Photo courtesy of Clyde Vandivort and Paul Stein.*

her husband's sole disposal nor liable for his debts. Missouri would not follow the example of these other states until 1909.

Professor Barbara Glosner Fines, University of Missouri School of Law-Kansas City, writes:

> Historically, upon marriage a woman entered the condition of "coverture" in which her legal identity was merged with that of her husband. He acquired exclusive ownership of all personal property she owned or acquired before or during the marriage. In Missouri any real property either of them owned before marriage or that was acquired during the marriage was presumed to be held as tenants by the entireties—that is, it was owned by marital entity rather than either spouse individually, but the husband had the exclusive right to control the property.

Although I was surprised at Julia's provision for Mattie Peterman in the codicil to her will, back in 1872, Mattie's parents had set up a similar instrument. On their wedding day, Mattie and Linus Sanford agreed to and signed a marriage contract as follows:

> On the 31st day of January 1872, Martha J. Russell of the first part and Linus Sanford of the second part and Charles Russell and J.G. Russell of the third part executed the following instrument: Whereas a marriage is agreed on and intended to be solemnized between the party of the first part and the party of the second part and on the treaty of said marriage it was agreed by and between them: That all property of any kind whatever in the County of Cape Girardeau or elsewhere which she is entitled to and which may at any time hereafter before or during her coverture fall to her by gift, devise, inheritance in course of distribution or otherwise howsoever in her own right should be conveyed, assigned and settled to her own sole and separate use during her coverture free from any control by or liability for or an account of her said intended husband and subject to be disposed of by her appointment of direction.

The document went on to cover the large estate left to her by her father as well as instructions for the trustees and provisions for her issue. It was signed by Linus, Martha Jane, and T.J. Russell, trustee.

When Mary Frizel Russell wrote her will, she inserted no less than six times a clause protecting the female heirs' property rights.

Julia Adele Vandivort with DAR pin. *Photo courtesy of Clyde Vandivort and Paul Stein.*

To her daughter Martha Jane Sanford, she gave her house and lots in Jackson "for her sole and separate use, and free from any claim control and interest thereof and therein of her husband." To Julia E. Harris, she bequeathed her house and lot on the levee in Range D in Cape Girardeau "for her sole and separate use, free from the claim, interest, or control thereof and therein of her husband." To her female grandchildren, she willed one-fourth of her lots in St. Louis, which came from her deceased husband, "free from any claim, control, and interest thereof and therein of any husband they may have." To her three children, Martha J. Sanford, Julia E. Harris, and James W. Russell, she bequeathed the farm on Crooked Creek near White Water Station in Cape Girardeau County, which she inherited from her father Joseph Frizel and the heirs of Frizel and Ranney, three-fourths of the undivided lots in St. Louis, and all of her lots in the town of Bird's Point, Missouri, with the exception in each bequest that her two daughters be "free from any claim, interest, and control thereof or therein of their respective husbands."

When I examined George F. Bollinger's will in the Cape Girardeau County Recorder's office in Jackson, filed October 9, 1843, I realized that he had established the precedent safeguarding the Bollinger women when he made the first trust in the family back in 1842 in order to protect his daughter Sarah in two areas. First, he wanted Sarah to receive ownership of all his land, the mill, and all his other possessions upon his death without the danger of it passing into the hands of her spouse; however, married women could not own property. In addition, he feared that his son-in-law, Ralph Daugherty, would gain control of the land and give it to the Vincentians, since Ralph had previously sold his choice property to the Catholics in Cape Girardeau at what seemed to the family quite a low price. (The earlier section entitled "Sarah and Ralph Daugherty" details the mounting dissension between George Bollinger and Ralph Daugherty.)

So on August 25, 1842, George set up his plan to circumvent Ralph's claim to Sarah's property. He began his will:

> In the name of God Amen. I, George F. Bollinger being of sound mind and disposing memory and believing it necessary to make a final disposition of all my worldly affairs, do make this my last will and testament. The consequence of the marriage of my only child and daughter Sarah with Ralph Daugherty, it had become extremely difficult to make a disposition

of my property for the benefit of my said daughter and her children (Elizabeth Frizzell, Mary Frizzell, Sarah Josephine Frizzell, George Frederick Daugherty, Samuel Daugherty, and Bernice Daugherty) in such a manner that the said Ralph Daugherty cannot have any, in trust either directly or indirectly therein or in anyway to have control or benefit by the same, I hereby declare it my intention for the preservation of my said daughter and her said children to make such a disposition of my property…that the said Ralph Daugherty shall …even be as a stranger.

To effect this intent, George bequeathed all he possessed (lands, real estate, cattle, hogs, horses, Negroes, farming utensils, household furniture, kitchen furniture, and all other property) to Charles Welling, Franklin Cannon, and Ralph Guild, who would serve as trustees, managing the estate for Sarah and her children and providing for her needs out of the estate funds as may be necessary.

In an additional item George added the following stipulation:

In case the marriage now existing between Ralph Daugherty and my daughter Sarah should hereafter in any way be dissolved and my daughter become a *femme sole* [a female who is divorced, never married, or is a widow and thus able to own property], in that case all my estate personal real and mixed moneys effects *et al.* shall go direct to my said daughter who will have hold and enjoy the same during natural life and at her death to be equally divided up between the said children of my said daughter then living, share and share alike. . . . My said daughter individually will exercise the rights powers and enjoy the benefit mentioned without reference to Ralph Daugherty, who is not to have any interest therein or control in the matter, being as effectually debarred from having any control or power interest now or hereafter as much as if the said Ralph Daugherty had never been married to my said daughter or was now effectually divorced.

George's provision herein to protect his daughter's interest in her property established the pattern for future wills in the Bollinger family.

Julia Adele Sanford Vandivort. *Photo courtesy of Clyde Vandivort and Paul Stein.*

Epilogue:

And the Julias Go On

On the day that I took that first trip to the Cape Girardeau County Archives in Jackson, I began what I thought was a simple project—to find out about the little house that is in the basement of our big house, but now two years later I am amazed at the Missouri history I have learned as I read about each period of time in the life of Julia and her family, covering a span of 156 years from 1799–1955. From the time in junior high when I first checked out from the library a Nancy Drew mystery, I have read hundreds of detective novels and have become addicted to finding clues and solving mysteries. The first clues in my search for Julia, which launched my treasure hunt, were handed to me in the form of probate files at the Cape Girardeau County Archives.

Over the next two years, I looked at old tax records and probate files, finding the original promissory note Joseph Russell signed to purchase the lot at 313 Themis Street, the wills of both Joseph Russell and Julia Russell Harris, and much more at the Cape Girardeau County Archives. I searched for tombstones in cemeteries in Cape Girardeau, Jackson, and Burfordville and researched the old records of Christ Episcopal Church in Cape Girardeau and Church of the Redeemer in Jackson. I toured the Red House of Louis Lorimier. In Jackson I saw Sarah Bollinger's piano in the Oliver House and took pictures of Sarah and Joseph Frizel's house. I spent hours in the genealogy room of the Cape Girardeau City Library, exploring documents, reading entries from the Federal Writers' Project, and examining microfilm records from the State Archives. I corresponded with Susan Rehkopf, an archivist with the Episcopal Diocese in St. Louis. I saw Mattie Russell Sanford's wedding dress on display at the Cape River Heritage Museum. In the Recorder's Office in Jackson, I found George Bollinger's will and Ralph Daugherty's land transaction selling his prime real estate to the Vincentians. I visited Bollinger Mill and traveled to Perryville to tour St. Mary's of the Barrens, where the 1818 log cabin of Father Rosati, the church begun in 1827, and the seminary built in 1837 still stand. I drove to St. Louis to find buildings designed by Jerome Legg. I read 150-year-old newspapers and viewed the Henry Flad display on the Civil War at the Southeast Missouri State University Archives. In Kent Library, I read historians Houck, Goodspeed, Flint, Bollinger, Shrum, Conard, Douglass, and Boyer and researched the seventy-volume military records of the Civil War, along with General Grant's memoirs and letters. I visited Fort D and the dungeon underneath Common Pleas Courthouse, where Linus Sanford was imprisoned during the Civil War. I read *Clyde and Julia Sanford Vandivort of Cape Girardeau, Missouri, Their Ancestors and Descendants* and the old minutes of the Cape Girardeau Board of Education proceedings when Julia Vandivort was the first woman to serve on the board. Following the path of Charles Russell, I visited the Charles Marion Russell Museum in Great Falls, Montana. At all stages of my research I gathered pictures of people, places, and documents with my camera.

In my attempt to understand what would have been happening in Julia's family, as I researched her family's lives in the different historical periods, the Bollingers, Frizels, Daughertys, Russells, Sanfords, Williamses, Harrises, and Vandivorts became my adopted family. And in my attempt to find Julia, the first lady of 313 Themis, I not only found Julia Harris but also many more Julias.

At the July 3, 2005, Vandivort reunion, Harriet Stein Smith, daughter of Julia Sanford Vandivort Stein, addressed the group by saying: "I want every Julia in the room to stand up. Do you know who you were named for? I bet most of you would say we trace the name back to Julia Sanford Vandivort, my grandmother. Well, SHE was named for her Aunt Julia . . . Julia Elizabeth Russell Harris." Just a few of the other Julias are: Julia Sanford Vandivort Stein, Julia Jane Smith Koenig, Julia Johnson, Julie Vandivort, Julia Marie Levin, Julia Alexander Smith, Julia Vandivort Roundy, and Julia Adele Sanford Vandivort. There is even a Julian.

So I began with a Julia and I'm ending with a Julia. And the Julias will go on. But the little house in the big house still remains a mystery.

Kaye Smith Hamblin
March 26, 2012

Acknowledgments

As I look back over the years when I was searching for Julia, I remember my first trip to the Cape Girardeau County Archives in Jackson and the awe I felt when I held the original promissory note written in 1850 for the land on which Julia's house would someday be built. That historical find drew me back to the archives many times, where Steven Pledger and Andrew Blattner were the first in a long list of people who helped me find information. In Jackson I also made numerous visits to the Cape County Recorder's office, where I was able to find helpful clues on land ownership.

Lisa Sanders, the church secretary at Christ Episcopal Church, patiently allowed me to pore over the church records in which I found documentation for the two children of Samuel and Julia Harris; records of baptisms, deaths, and marriages; and minutes of the Christ Church Guild. Dr. Bonnie Stepenoff encouraged my writing in the writers' workshops held at the Cape River Heritage Museum, as well as located for me Mattie Sanford's original wedding dress and Mattie's and Linus Sanford's pictures in the museum's collections. Kyle Mabuce of the Jackson Heritage Association provided information about Sarah Bollinger, while Cathi Stoverink helped me search the Association's large collection of older pictures from Cape County.

The Episcopal Diocese archivist Susan Rehkopf from St. Louis found passages from the 1821 bishop's journal and notes in the *Church News* about the early history of the Church of the Redeemer in Jackson. She also supplied me with Russell family connections in St. Louis. Park rangers at Bollinger Mill first told me about Ralph Daugherty and his involvement with the Catholic Church in the Cape area, opening up a new chapter in my book. Ron Kirby provided the picture of St. Vincent's Seminary, photographed about 1890. Deborah Moseley assisted with the genealogical research.

From the Cape Board of Education came the minutes from meetings and an original ballot from 1922 when Julia Vandivort, the first woman to be elected to an office in Cape, was serving on the board. The librarians of the Cape Girardeau Public Library aided my research by ordering microfilms from the Missouri State Archives and making a wide range of historical materials available in the Genealogy room. Among these materials was Edison Shrum's collection on slavery in Cape County, which offered interesting insights. Dr. Lisa

Speer and her staff at Special Collections and Archives at Southeast Missouri State University were an invaluable help in providing access to relevant collections, as well as information on the Civil War in Cape Girardeau.

I owe a special debt of gratitude to Paul Stein for the use of his document *Clyde and Julia Sanford Vandivort of Cape Girardeau, Missouri, Their Ancestors and Descendants*, and to Paul Stein and Clyde Vandivort for their family pictures.

Dr. Susan Swartwout, director of the Southeast Missouri University Press, without whom Julia's book would not have been published, and her assistant, Carrie M. Walker, spent many hours expertly assembling the pictures and text.

Of course, I must thank my husband Bob, who accompanied me on many treasure hunts, always encouraging me in my research and writing.

Finally, I am most grateful to Julia Russell Harris for the legacy she left, including the house she and her husband Samuel planned and built at 313 Themis Street, where our family now has the privilege to live and enjoy a rich historical heritage.

—Kaye Smith Hamblin